STORYTELLER

Outline From Vision to Finish
Losing the Ma

BY

M HAROLD PAGE

COPYRIGHT

ISBN-13:978-1519755193
ISBN-10:1519755198
©M Harold Page 2014
All rights reserved.

Acknowledgements: My friends have provided invaluable support, encouragement and beta reading. My world, it seems, is full of writers.

Contents

1. **CRAFT AND VISION** 6
   - CRAFT AND VISION: SUMMARY 9
2. **FIRST, LEARN TO TOUCH TYPE** 10
   - FIRST, LEARN TO TOUCH TYPE: SUMMARY 11
3. **INTRODUCING MY WRITING TOOLSET** 12
   - STORY SCULPTING TOOLS 13
   - STORYTELLING TOOLS 15
   - USE YOUR STORYTELLER INSTINCT 16
   - INTRODUCING MY WRITING TOOLSET: SUMMARY 18
4. **STORY SCULPTING TOOLS** 19
   - CONFLICT DIAGRAM 19
     - *The "Snipers in the Belfries" Rule* 19
     - *Different Kinds of Conflict* 20
     - *Bone of Contention* 21
     - *How to draw a Conflict Diagram* 22
     - *The Conflict Diagram is the creative process* 24
     - *Conflict Diagrams are flexible* 25
     - *Conflict Diagrams and Worldbuilding* 29
     - *Notes and Pointers* 33
     - *Conflict Diagram Exercises* 34
   - STORY OUTLINE 34
     - *Outlines: You're doing it wrong* 34
     - *How to write a writable Story Outline* 35
     - *Expanding your Story Outline* 38
     - *Climax and Ending* 39
     - *Worldbuilding and the Story Outline* 40
     - *Story Outline Exercises* 41
   - STORY QABNS 41
     - *Introducing the QABN (pronounced "Cabin")* 42
     - *Using Story QABNs to understand your story* 44
     - *Using the Table of Doom to tighten the structure of your Story Outline* 48
     - *Using Story QABNs as a way in* 51

    Story QABN Exercises *54*
  BARBARIAN IN THE CITY 55
    First stab at the outline for Barbarian in the City *55*
    Story QABNs for Barbarian in the City *60*
    Tinkering with the Story Outline and the Story QABNs *61*
  STORY SCULPTING TOOLS: SUMMARY 63
  STORY SCULPTING TOOLS: EXERCISES 63

5. STORYTELLING TOOLS 64

  CHAPTER OUTLINE 64
    How to write a Chapter Outline *64*
    How to tell if there is enough plot in your chapter *65*
    Worldbuilding in the Chapter Outline *69*
    Chapter Outline Exercises *70*
  SCENE QABNS 70
    How to write a Scene QABN *71*
    Debate Scenes *73*
    Final thoughts: Parallel narratives *74*
    Worldbuilding with Scene QABNs *75*
    Scene QABNs Exercises *75*
  SCENE OUTLINES 76
    How to write a Scene Outline *76*
    Worldbuilding in the Scene Outline *77*
    Scene Outlines Exercises *78*
  STORYTELLING TOOLS: SUMMARY 78
  STORYTELLING TOOLS: EXERCISES 78

6. DRAFTING THE TEXT 79

  THE WORLD/CHARACTER DIALOGUE 79
    Prerequisites for using World/Character Dialogue *81*
    How to use the World/Character Dialogue *81*
    Editing, Expanding and Contracting World/Character Dialogs *84*
    Worldbuilding during drafting *85*
  DRAFTING: SUMMARY 86
  DRAFTING EXERCISES 86

7. FINAL WORD 87

1. CRAFT AND VISION

At the time of writing, I've written *and sold* three short Historical adventure novels inside one calendar year, and started the new year by doing the same with a fourth.

By *written* I mean *written from scratch*. I went from, "You want me to write a story set in the Wars of the Roses? OMG, where do I sign?" to "Glad you like the final draft. Thanks for the money!" inside three (3) months working a 20-hour a week (in theory; less if you allow for children randomly underfoot due to holidays and sickness, and occasionally infesting my sword-lined study to play Minecraft).

You see, I make my living as a writer of franchise fiction. I write novels to "tie in" with—at the moment—existing series and computer games. This isn't hackwork. Nowadays, editors take their franchises seriously and demand proper novels with characterisation, themes, pacing and plot, and all the stuff your old English Lit teacher told you about. However, the editors also demand speed and reliability. It's no good signing to deliver something in three months, then finally delivering three years later with tales of angst and writer's block.

I couldn't have managed this five years ago.

My ideas always come to me top-down as intense but vague visions of the novel I want to write: "*Yeah. Spaceships and dragons. The galaxy. The emptiness of space… Ninja girls in shiny silver jumpsuits…*" Or: *"Knights…! Mayhem…! Tanks…! Magic!"* Sometimes, as with my franchise books, all I have to go on is an existing setting: *"Wars of the Roses! Go!"*

If you're like me, then your initial vision is big picture, or an impression of what you want to achieve. This could, for instance, be some literary cluster of thoughts: *"History…! Russia…! Art….! Meaning…!"*, slice-of life-ish impressions: *"Clogs…! Mills…! Patriarchy…!"* or a world you love, whether a historical milieu or a roleplaying setting.

If you *are* like me—and I'm guessing you are because you're still reading this—then, when you sit down to *write* that novel, the vision melts away. Your storyteller instinct rejects your every effort. You can only spend so long staring at a blank screen or typing round in circles, so sooner or later you abandon the book and the vision.

That's how I ended up with a dozen sets of first three chapters scattered across half a dozen hard drives and floppy disks (remember those?) since I was fifteen. I can't show these to you because I binned them. Once I learned to craft a proper story, my early efforts lost their significance, except perhaps as inspiration for new ones.

I used the term "craft" as writers do, as if the craft was the whole story. But that's like saying that the very vital construction workers and engineers are the whole story behind a prominent public building. The (hard-won, in my case) truth is that the craft of writing exists only to turn our inner vision into something we can share with others.

That inner vision thing is a little embarrassing, and certainly not very British. We don't really talk about it. My fellow writers tend to squirm when the subject comes up. However, it is why we write. That is why if you focus too much on craft, you end up with a joyless construction exercise. However, focus too much on vision and you have tripe (and perhaps a shrill sense of entitlement: "my voice deserves to be heard!"). The trick, however, is not to balance them, but to get them to work together. I do this by trusting my storyteller instinct.

Though it's hard to create a story out of thin air, we all know what a story should look like. It's a human thing. A story either strikes a chord—raises hairs on the nape of our necks—or it does not. This innate knowledge, this storyteller instinct, is what screams at novice writers that we are writing crap. That's where 90% of issues with Writer's Block, the Internal Editor, and Resistance come from.

Conventional wisdom, citing author James Rollins, is to "give yourself permission to write crap". This works. Ignore the naysaying voices and just write through the pain, then hone, then rewrite. Eventually you may evolve a novel. It has the twin advantages of making a very airy-fairy pursuit feel macho, and of giving you lots of opportunity for very public self-hate, the which requires much less effort than actually finishing a book.

However, "permission to write crap" has two problems. First, it's time-consuming and, thus, often soul-destroying. All that rewriting can leave you hating the work that was once your *magnum opus*. Second, and more importantly, it only works if you have some idea what to write in the first place. Some of us start off with a vision which isn't an opening scene, or a character in conflict. How do we "just write"?

My alternative is to not to "not write crap", but to bring the vision into focus in stages and from different angles, and then to test the results. If it's "crap", I tinker or try again, but the agony lasts minutes or hours, not days and months.

To put it another way, I try to nail down some aspect of the novel—the broad story, the characters or conflicts—and see whether my storyteller instinct is excited by it. If it passes muster, I move onto another aspect.

This has major advantages.

First, it's fun: spawning, then rejecting, then respawning possible novels with dizzying speed.

Second, it's economical. Each change of direction, each new attempt, involves scrubbing a handful of words, not chapters.

Third, it's fast. This is obviously a professional necessity, and also useful if you're trying to break into fiction while writing in the gaps in your life. But it's also immensely spiritually satisfying to finish a work and move onto the next. I don't know about you, but I have more novels to write than I have years left on this planet!

In learning to do this, I have honed six simple creativity tools plus an effective approach to drafting text. That's what this book is about.

This is a handbook. No formulas, not much literary theory, no padding with little folksy tales of my life, and no attempt to inspire and enthuse you. I'm not even going to try to sell you on my approach; try it and make up your own mind.

If the result seems a little short, consider that this book is a hell of a lot cheaper than all those tempting writer's retreats and conferences.

Craft and Vision: Summary

o Though we pretend not, most writers write in order to express some kind of creative vision.
o Even so, modern novels are big and fat and require planning.
o The best planning tools let you see your novel from different perspectives and then respond to it creatively using your storyteller instinct.
o My planning tools work for me. Perhaps they will work for you.

2. FIRST, LEARN TO TOUCH TYPE

Seriously. Barn-dancing your fingers around the keyboard will only take you so far.

Go find an online typing course (The Children's BBC website has a good free one where talking animals will irritate you into excellence). Don't forget to sort out your ergonomics. Sitting wrong for intense typing sessions will break you, and that will cost you word count.

Don't think it's just about knocking out word count! There are artistic reasons.

Your word processor isn't just a tool for *recording* your thoughts, it's an extra space—a sandbox—for *thinking* those thoughts. If you can't type at the speed you think then, at best, the physical act of typing is holding you back, like trying to make sandcastles while wearing boxing gloves. At worst, it's turning the whole writing process into a physical chore. Creativity belongs to the inner child, and children don't like chores.

Also, you need to be able to treat your text with the detachment of a 5-year-old who is prepared to kick over a dozen sandcastles in order to make better ones. If a scene doesn't work, then there is usually something wrong with the structure of the novel that supports that scene and thousands of words must go. If your writing is reasonably tight, with every word counting as part of the whole, it's not even worth going back to rescue nice bits of description. You can only have faith in your ability to pull the same trick again. It's emotionally easier to do this if it doesn't take you hours to type all those words.

Finally, the techniques set out in this handbook involve typing; lots of typing, and mostly "in flow". If you approach typing grudgingly, if you unconsciously bemoan the effort expended in each keystroke, then this will all seem like too much hard work. You might as well go play *Skyrim* instead.

However, if you can type with the same ease you talk, then you can use my techniques with the kind of creative fervour normally reserved for abstract artists hurling paint pots around.

So, learn to touch type. Trust me, it's liberating.

First, Learn To Touch Type: Summary

Learn to touch type:
- It's more fun.
- Encourages you to treat your text as disposable.
- Removes unconscious barriers.

3. INTRODUCING MY WRITING TOOLSET

So, you have a vision, a backwards echo or pre-memory of your novel. But what kind of vision?

Think of what you remember of novels that *already* exist. What sticks with you long after you read the book?

Sometimes it's the conflict between opposing forces, like George RR Martin's *Game of Thrones*. Sometimes it's the high-concept story world, like Charles Stross's *Family Trade*. Sometimes it's the richly textured twisty-turny plot, like Patrick Rothfuss's *Name of the Wind*... Sometimes it's the main character, like in Jim Butcher's *Harry Dresden* books. Sometimes it's the story itself, like Tolkien's *The Hobbit*, or *Beowulf*.

Different novels leave you with different kinds of memory. In the same way, different potential works of fiction grant you different kinds of vision. That's why I can't offer One True Process for Writing a Novel. Instead, I have six tools that you can apply in any order, depending on what kind of vision you have:

Story Sculpting	**Storytelling**
Conflict Diagrams	Chapter Outline
Story QABNs	Scene QABNs
Story Outlines	Scene Outlines
TEXT	

I've grouped them according to two different kinds of writerly activity: Story Sculpting and Storytelling. Each of these also applies to "Worldbuilding", the process by which we research and/invent our story world. However, I'll deal with that when I go into each tool in detail.

I'm going to use the rest of this chapter to briefly introduce you to these tools and their uses, since it helps to see them together before going over them one at a time.

Story Sculpting Tools

Story Sculpting
Conflict Diagrams
Story QABNs
Story Outlines

Story Sculpting often starts in the pub, or on a long walk, or over coffee. It's when we go blurry eyed and… *remember…* the novel we are about to write, then try and explain it while waving our arms and knocking over beer glasses—I mean, *disturbing the crows as we wander lonely and angst-ridden through wintery lanes*. We taste different possible futures for our novel, and as our vision firms up, get a sense of its final shape.

Story Sculpting is holistic, non-linear. We deal with the whole novel at one go as if moulding a lump of clay to match our vision. However, whereas clay has three dimensions, a novel has as many as you care to identify. Clearly, we need to simplify the task, not by simplifying the novel, but rather by working on it from one perspective at a time. The perspectives I find most useful are conflicts, story questions, and outlines.

Conflicts are what drive a story and engage the reader. By "conflict" I mean *any* interesting relationship in which one character or force struggles with another over an interesting issue. By interesting, I mean whatever fires you up when you think about it.

Conflicts can be as violent as French versus English, but they can also be between people and almost any obstacle, e.g. their own disability, the environment, patriarchy, class, the uncaring world… Some conflicts get resolved in the story. Others just form part of the setting and thus impact on the story. However, without conflicts to resolve, you have no story… *you knew that right?* This is why it's important to know your conflicts.

I explore the conflicts in my novels using **Conflict**

Diagrams, a simple diagrams that nail down who or what is struggling over what. You may find these useful if your vision feels rather static—an existing story world, a seeming utopia, or a quirky cast of characters—or if you are interested in grand sweeping conflicts and need to discover some more personal ones to drive a story.

Story questions are what generate suspense, and keep the reader reading: *Will our hero get the girl? Will the aliens come? Who did the murder? What happens next?* Usually the most compelling questions relate to a conflict: *Will the hero beat the enemy? Will the hero get through the desert?* Story questions also articulate themes (Wooo! Literary!); *Is there a God? What is love? Which is better, revenge or forgiveness?* Finally, the answers to these questions are what create satisfying climaxes and endings (of which, more later).

I have adopted a formal way of setting out story questions, Question-Answer-But-Now; hence the name of the tool, **Story QABNs** (pronounced "cabins"). You may find these useful if you have a strong sense of how your characters start the story, but not much idea of what happens next.

An outline tells us what happens in the story. It reveals the chain of cause and effect and the timetabling required to get from the beginning to the end. Though there's certainly no single way to write an outline, there are certainly some wrong ones.

An outline must be more than just a laundry list itinerary—rescue the princess, kill the dragon, save the ninja temple—it has to read like a riveting yarn in its own right so that we can test it against our instincts. For this reason, I write a **Story Outline** using a rhythm of action-reaction, cause-effect. If you need to discover by writing, then an Outline may save you days, weeks, or years, since it has the advantage of fitting onto one page. If you write yourself into a corner then you need only bin, say, 200 words and not 20,000.

Storytelling Tools

Storytelling
Chapter Outline
Scene QABNs
Scene Outlines

For a writer, Storytelling is the actual process behind typing the text.

It's when you chart a course over the surface of the squirming living thing you created during Story Sculpting.

Novices obsess over word counts. However, the actual wordage is the tip of the iceberg; the story has to be chopped into chapters and scenes, and the scenes themselves must have some kind of meaningful shape.

Like building a sandcastle, Storytelling is a mostly linear activity dealing in detail: A leads to B leads to C and so on. However, also like making a sandcastle, some shaping of individual components is required—we always do our sandcastles with outer walls, towers, and moats—oftentimes requiring a major rethink. I usually come to Storytelling after I have finished Story Sculpting. However, some people and some novels work best at this level and the tools set out here reflect this.

Chapters—rather than acts, by the way—are the building blocks of a novel. The **Chapter Outline** is just the Story Outline refined to describe each chapter. Depending on your genre, you quickly get the feeling for how much needs to go into each chapter. This can be important for knowing if you have enough story to fill your book. However, this can also be a first point of entry to the entire novel. If you can "see" the start of your novel in detail, and tend to think in concrete specifics, try writing a Chapter Outline.

Scenes are what make up chapters. Theatrical theory demands unity of time and place, but we're not thespians! Instead a scene asks a question and answers it, usually moving the story forward. For this reason, I use what I call a **Scene QABN** (remember, "Question-Answer-But-Now") to structure each and every scene: "Can the shelter-seeking hero break into the old barn? Yes, but he finds a body. Now he must decide what to do." Setting out the Scene QABN is a good test of whether or not the scene is actually interesting. If it's boring, you probably need to come up with a different scene. If your vision is of a story that's something of a random walk, then you may want to actually start out by creating a string of Scene QABNs.

I also use **Scene Outlines.** These may not be to your taste, or may just exist in your head, but I find it useful to set out what happens in a scene before drafting it. It's just a blow-by-blow summary of the scene that enables me to relax and enjoy the drafting, and, since I am lazy, I have an easy way of setting this out.

As for the drafting itself; working in flow is great, but as with jamming jazz or fighting in a martial arts style, there are techniques that are good to internalise. By the time you've finished editing your text, you will end up with a kind of rhythm, so you might as well get into the habit of writing like that anyway. I'll show you how to do that nearer the end.

Use your Storyteller Instinct

The most important tool is the one I have not listed: your storyteller instinct.

All my six tools do is let me interrogate my vision and hold the result up to the light so I can find out whether or not I like it.

I don't, for example, stare at a Chapter Outline, rub my sword scar and decide if it's "technically perfect". Instead, I let my imagination whirl around inside it, giving me hints of the scenes I'll write, and go, "Whoa! That is cool!"

Though the tools are part of the creative process, they are not the actual story. Rather, they are a view of it, like the graphs so beloved of economists and sales professionals. For example, if my Conflicts Diagram shows two characters in conflict, then that's something I *know* about the characters themselves. I never think, "*The diagram shows Peter and Jane have a conflict.*"

Also, this is neither a software methodology nor an instruction leaflet for assembling flat-pack furniture. Though I've presented these tools in a logical hierarchy, you don't have to work with them in that order. Instead, trust your storyteller instinct to tell you when to put down one tool and pick up another.

Typically, I start with a bit of Story Outline, then come up with a Conflict Diagram and some related Story QABNs, then return to the Story Outline and then work on the Chapter Outline, discover new conflicts and go back to the Conflict Diagram... it's no different from fixing a washing machine or installing shelves; I don't do the entire job with just my electrical screwdriver.

So, there is no fixed process or even steady flow. However you begin, you inevitably end up bouncing between tools like a pinball in an earthquake. There is no right way to write other than to trust your instincts. It's different between writers and between novels. Whatever works is good!

Finally, don't be tempted to turn this into a documentation exercise. You aren't commenting code, filling out a tax form, or justifying design decisions to third parties! Your story will be judged on its text alone. These are just useful tools. Turn them into the entire point of the exercise, and your storyteller instinct will vanish like the Elves from Middle Earth (or was it Hyboria?).

Introducing My Writing Toolset: Summary

o "Story Sculpting" is when you shape the entire novel.
o "Storytelling" is when you take what you have and make it into a linear story.
o I have six tools for these activities, which you can use in any order.

4. STORY SCULPTING TOOLS

Story Sculpting	Storytelling
Conflict Diagrams	Chapter Outline
Story QABNs	Scene QABNs
Story Outlines	Scene Outlines
TEXT	

Story Sculpting is what I called it when you deal with the shape and dynamic of your entire story. It's the most logical place to start an explanation. However, remember that the order in which you use these tools depends entirely on the vision that's rattling around in your head and on what your instincts say. It's entirely reasonable, say, to "free-write" three chapters during the small hours of the morning after a particularly good party, then come to Story Sculpting tools in order to work out how to write the rest of the book. To repeat the mantra; *trust your storyteller instinct.*

Conflict Diagram

Story *is* conflict, or at least conflict and resolution. (Though it should have been blindingly obvious, the need for conflict explains the abject failure of so many of my youthful writing projects. As a pissed-off teenager, I wrote for escape, and in escaping tended to imagine conflict-free utopias. Don't make this mistake!)

Before we get to the actual diagrams, let me drive this home by introducing you to a rule I discovered…

The "Snipers in the Belfries" Rule

If you want the reader to *notice* your beautifully described belfries, then you must put snipers in them! Here's why.

Readers only really "see" things that are part of a conflict. They experience any description you just slip in as:

> Blah blah blah blah blah. Blah blah. Blah blah blah blah. **Characters do something at last.**

However, you can still get them to notice your beautifully described belfries as long as you put snipers in them:

> A movement on the roof drew Olaf's eye. He squinted into the glare and frowned. The sun had turned the forest of belfries into jagged silhouettes. What with all those gargoyles and ornamental projections, there was no way of knowing how many snipers were up there. He toggled his communicator. "Air strike at the following coordinates."

In a nutshell, if you want to dump your scenery into people's imaginations, then have people fight *to* it, fight *for* it, or fight *in/on* it. This is how Tolkien made his landscape porn work in *The Hobbit*. For example, the party battled through Middle Earth *to* the Lonely Mountain, struggled *for* possession of it, then fought a battle *on* its slopes.

Different Kinds of Conflict

Conflict, of course, doesn't need to be about actual physical combat. Go back to the belfries. Perhaps the story is a modern romantic comedy focused on the effort to restore some Medieval belfries and the protagonist must convince people of their worth, get involved in the actual work, and maybe strike up a romance with the stonemason.

Like belfries, characters only really come alive in their conflicts with other characters, their environment and themselves—hence all those buddy movies with mismatched characters finding friendship, and those "opposites attract" comedy romances. Hence also Gimli and Legolas.

This explains why some real-life stories stick in our heads or enter mythology. Take Albert Ball, the WWI British fighter ace. He was very good at shooting down Germans. However, what makes him memorable is that he liked to visit them in hospital if they survived, and that he grew flowers outside his tent; the doomed young man's vocation was in conflict with his gentle nature. Did I say "doomed young man"? There's another conflict, this time Youth vs Death.

There is, of course, no need to be crass about it and the best conflicts are ones that are "on topic" for the story. Not every police detective has to be battling with alcohol or a stoner teenage daughter. But what conflicts you choose for your story are down to your storyteller instinct. Just because everybody says something is a cliché doesn't mean to say that *you* can't make it fresh and interesting.

Conflict *can* be physical (Knights vs Tanks), but need not be. Typical story conflicts can be Social (Debutante vs Debutante), Romantic (Couple vs Forces Against Them), Mystery (Detective vs Mystery), Psychological (Writer vs Unbearable Angst), and Cultural (Chivalry vs Militarism).

It follows that the opposing—let's call them **Players**—in a conflict need be neither human nor even physically "real". Sometimes a conflict is between a character and a natural or social obstacle, e.g. Old Man vs the Sea, or Gentle Man vs Gender Stereotyping. (If the obstacle is boring, then so too will be your story.)

Bone of Contention

For a conflict to be useful for storytelling, we need to know more than just who the players are, we need to discover what the players think they are struggling over. What the **Bone of Contention** is.

We're not talking the underlying metaphor or the hidden

psychological truth! We just need to know what the players are ostensibly after.

Sometimes the Bone of Contention is a physical objective, e.g. possession of a fortress (as in Gemmell's *Druss the Legend*) or a physical object like a fish (as in Hemingway's *Old Man and the Sea*). In my Foreworld SideQuest *Marshal Versus the Assassins*, I used the famous Horn of Roland, the Oliphant he sounded at Roncesvalles.

Sometimes, though, the characters are wrestling over a complex relationship and whether or not it should exist (e.g. Austen's *Pride and Prejudice*.) It could even be an argument over how to frame a particular experience or person.

How to draw a Conflict Diagram

You may prefer to hold the conflicts in your head, or set them out anyway you want. Sometimes a simple list will do. An easy way of setting out the conflicts in a story is to use this form:

```
Player > Bone of Contention < Player
```

This gives us a list like this:

```
Hero > Fish < Sea
Hero > Fortress < Enemy
Hero > Relationship < Love Interest
```

However, I find basic diagramming software helps me capture the complexities of my story world. Open Office Draw, MS Word drawing tools, and MS Visio do this nicely if you are happy to use them. I use Scapple (from the same people who make Scrivener). You may want to use pencil and paper.

(By the way, for printable versions of all the illustrations, drop by **http://www.mharoldpage.com/**)

Here's an example of a conflict diagram from a novel I'm working on at the time of writing:

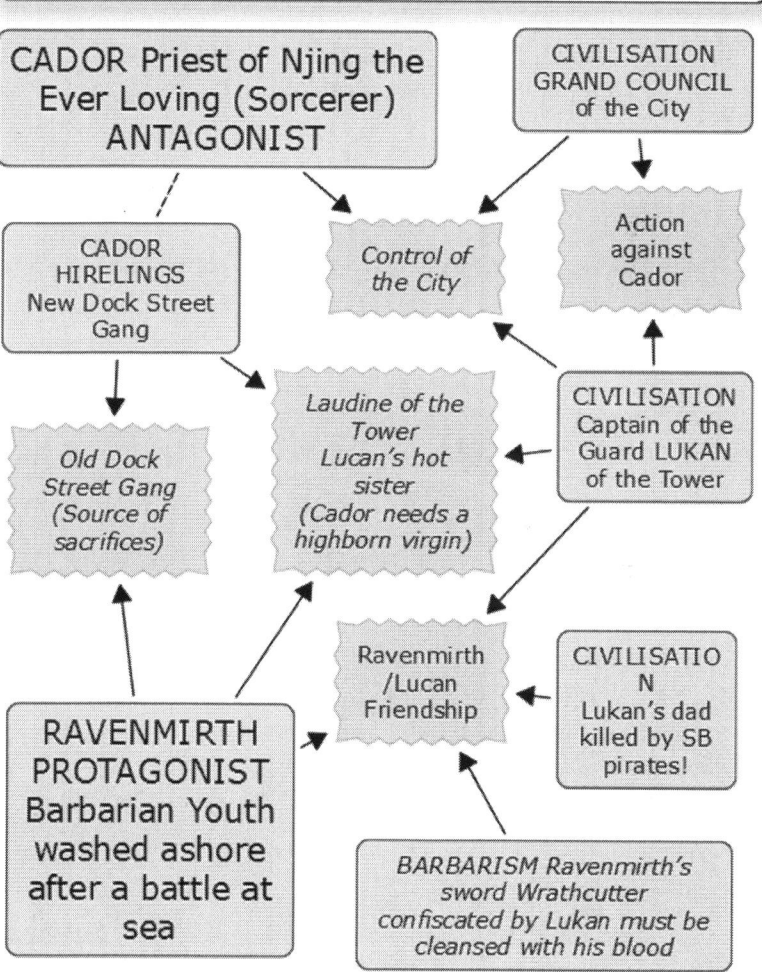

The arrows represent the conflicts.

I use broken lines to represent connections and alliances.

The boxes are the players: sometimes complex individuals, sometimes abstract forces personified as one or more individuals.

The jagged boxes with the italic text are Bones of Contention over which the players fight. (Note that this is just structural. In this example, both the *Old Dock Street Gang* and *Laudine of the Tower* are people in their own right, with hopes, dreams, objectives and agency.)

The Conflict Diagram is the creative process

Now here's the important bit.

The Conflict Diagram for *Barbarian in the City* doesn't capture or record the creative process, it *is* the creative process, or at least a brain add-on module that lets me wrestle with all these conflicts.

I had this vision of a YA Sword and Sorcery yarn. Ravenmirth, a Conan-like barbarian from the Sword Tribes, ends up marooned in a big decadent city (something like what would happen if Late Antique Alexandria, Justinian's Constantinople and Borgia Rome somehow merged).

So, this vague vision floating in my head, I added one player box for Ravenmirth and one for Cador the Sorcerer. I stared at it awhile and thought…

…*who would Ravenmirth fall in with first? Obviously a street gang. He could help them against another gang… what to call them? "Old Docks" and "New Docks"… Oh! The Old Docks could be silted up and derelict. Cool! Now where does Cador fit? Obviously he wants human sacrifices…*

The diagram began to get complicated. Then I realised Cador would hire the New Dock gang as his reapers—which my storyteller instinct liked—and the Old Dock gang became demoted to a Bone of Contention.

It happens that, having done a lot of reading about the 1930s for another project, I'm interested in the problem of how civilisation is vulnerable to those who don't play by the rules, which meant that it felt right that Civilisation should appear on the Conflict Diagram.

Wham! Somebody confiscates Ravenmirth's sword. Hello Captain Lukan, Civilisation personified! And that gives us his sister as a posh love interest. Ravenmirth and Laudine can meet when the barbarian tries to steal his sword back.

Oh! Oh! And of course, Cador kidnaps Laudine.

And then the rest fell into place as if the Muse had kicked down my door and taken over my computer.

The Grand Council is part paralysed by its own rules, and part by individual fear of Cador. Poor Lukan just can't get them to take action!

Finally, I needed to bring out the thematic stuff. I shifted the sword *Wrathcutter* from Bone of Contention to a personification of Barbarism *(yes I know, sword is not a person, but here, anything that's a player is also a person)* and created an uneasy friendship between the two male leads: the barbarian code demands that Ravenmirth slay Lukan for taking his sword; meanwhile, Lukan lost his dad to Sword Barbarian pirates so is not exactly keen on barbarians. Oh, and then there was the small matter of: what would persuade Ravenmirth to part with his precious sword rather than die defending it?

As I did all this, it was as if my "memory" of the finished book came back to me. The intellectual tool is there to support the artistic vision, not the other way around.

Looking at the diagram, it's a start. It'll grow with the telling—if I choose to write it! If I don't like the idea, I've merely wasted a couple of hours.

Conflict Diagrams are flexible

Now, barbarians and swords and mayhem—*those* are my thing. But just in case you think this method only works on crass larger-than-life-romps where people solve problems through the medium of interpersonal violence, here's something you might recognise:

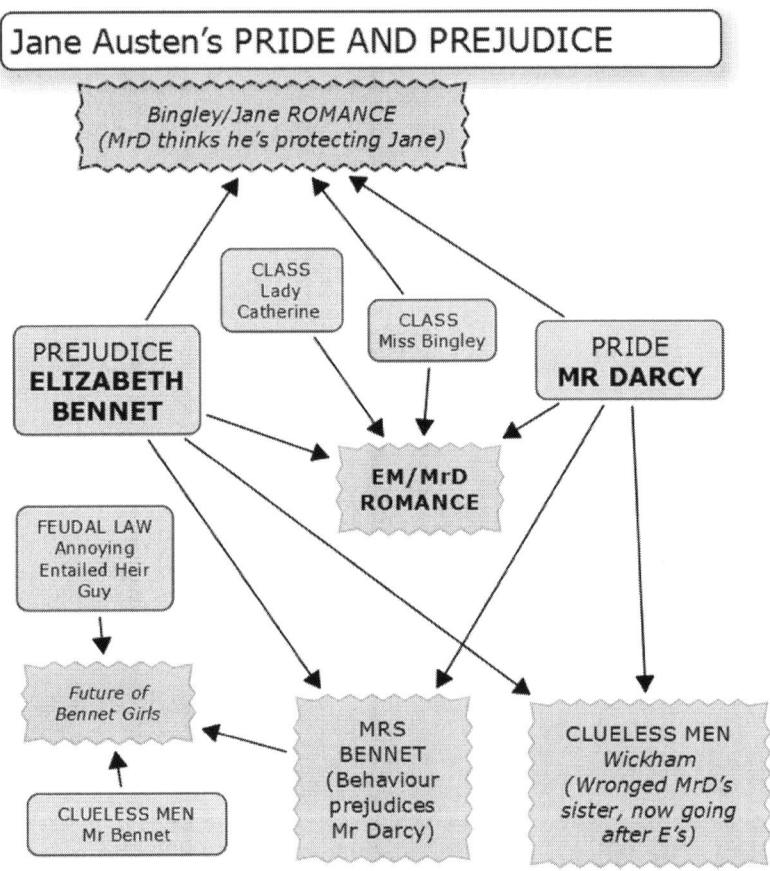

No, I don't think Jane Austen used a diagram like this! However, she *must* have had something like this in her head as she wrote. Look how many of the characters are Personified Forces! ("Clueless Men" who are therefore thoughtlessly cruel could be rolled up with "Feudal Law" and changed to "Patriarchy".)

Mrs Bennet is a Bone of Contention because Elizabeth and Darcy disagree about how to frame her behaviour. Elizabeth understands her mum is scared of poverty. Darcy just thinks the woman is an embarrassment. Mrs Bennet also has her own conflict over the Future of the Bennet Girls. I handled this by not italicising Mrs Bennet's box. (Whatever works!)

Note also that the two Romances are Bones of Contention. The shape or even existence of a Romance (or friendship, actually) is always going to be a Bone of Contention, even between enthusiastic lovers, and most certainly between the lovers and the outside forces.

Just for contrast, and to return to a genre I like, here's some *Sharpe*:

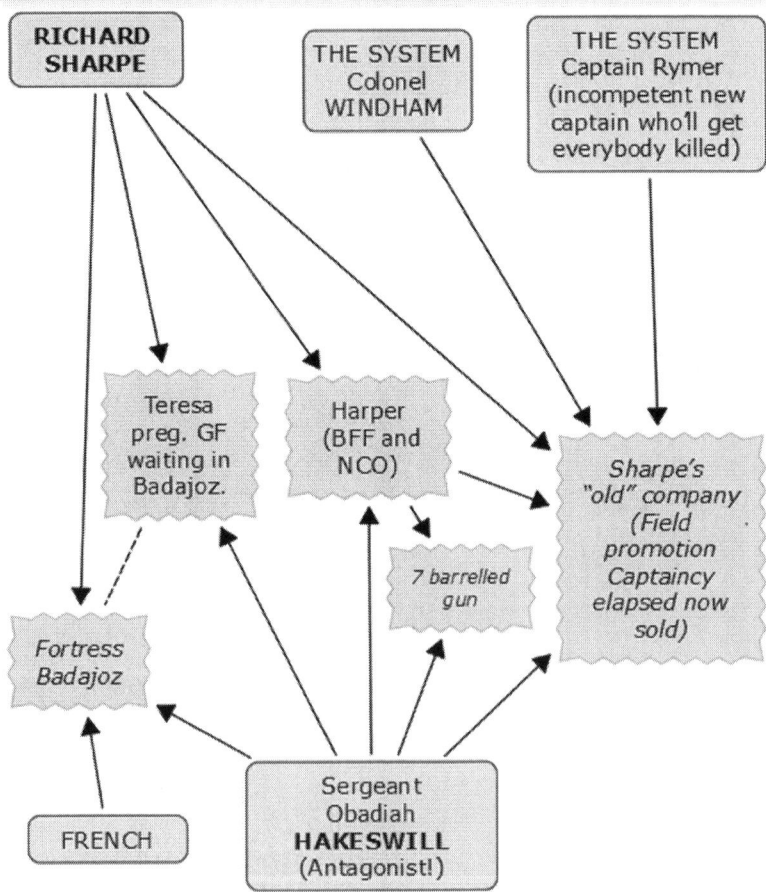

(Note that this diagram is set out like an actual working diagram using abbreviations. Your diagram is for you, not for anybody else.)

Like *Pride and Prejudice*, *Sharpe's Company* has personified forces and Bones of Contention—Harper and Teresa—who have their own conflicts. Essentially, though, all the Bones of Contention are really between Sharpe and Hakeswill. Just looking at the diagram tells me how tight a writer Cornwell is.

This kind of diagram is helpful with any kind of story.

Even if you know the setting well, making a diagram of what you know will spark more research or worldbuilding and steer you away from the clichéd obvious options, the overripe low-hanging fruit.

Conflict Diagrams and Worldbuilding

For me, Conflict Diagrams go from helpful to vital when I have to do **Worldbuilding** for a new setting. For example, here is what happened when I sat down to imagine an Industrial Revolution Steampunk setting.

I started just setting out the elements I'd learnt about from History: Industrialists, Workers, Old Aristocracy, Class System… Alas, the result looked no different from a Historical Novel, so dreamed up an external threat and got the Airship Nazis (note to self; *think of a better name…*):

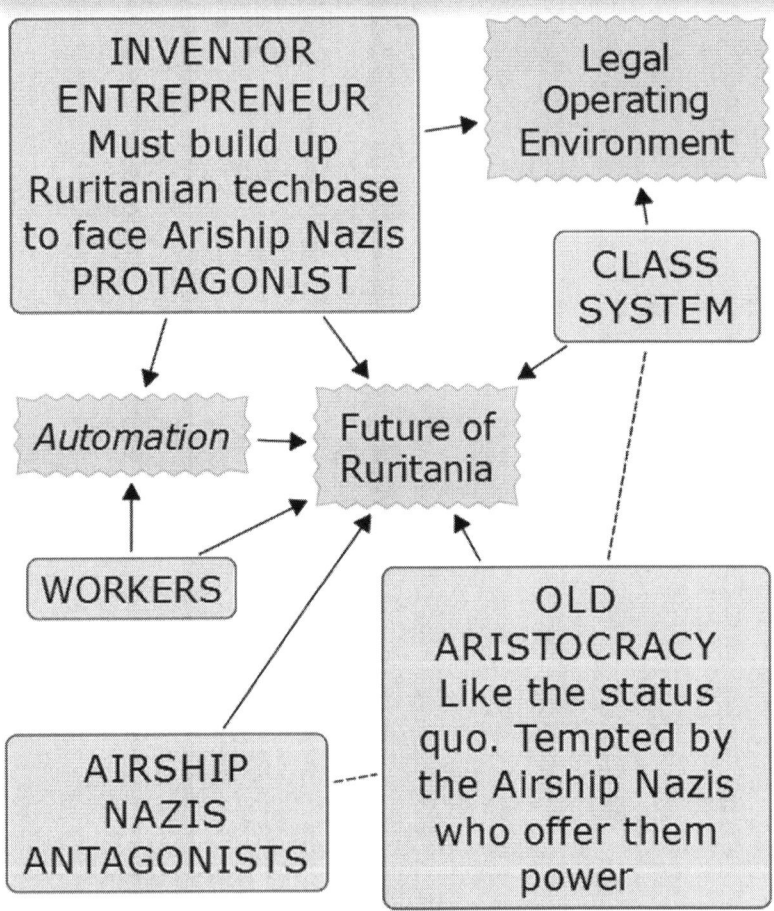

So far so good, but no people and hence no story! However, what I *have* captured are the main cultural and political conflicts in my story world. If your story was about an office romance, then you'd have quite different conflicts to do with, say, new technology, sexism and buyouts.

The important thing is to only go into as much detail as necessary. At this stage, I don't need a world map or history, nor do I need a detailed knowledge of airships. If I was writing a Historical Military yarn, I'd need to know the rough course of the relevant war and have a sense of what was going on in the respective armies and society, and that would be that. Similarly, in your Office Romance, you don't at this stage have to pick an industry or even a time period. This diagram tells you what you will need to research and/or invent. (Of course, reading widely and researching areas of interest is vital for fuelling your imagination.)

Having got a handle on the story world, it's time to start interrogating the circumstances and personifying the forces. This is what happened to my Steampunk world:

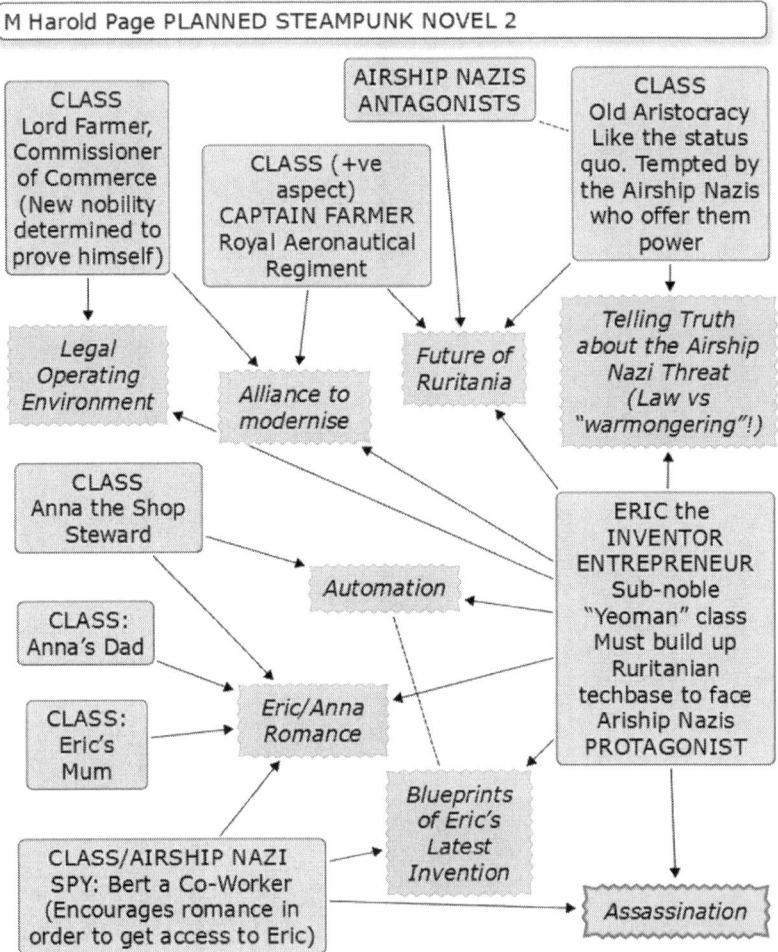

Honestly! This wasn't an intellectual exercise. It just grew, with visions of chases over factory roofs, spies, steamy romance...

Just in personifying the conflicts—dropping characters into the player boxes—and fleshing them out, I start to get a more vivid impression of the story world. Note that I've only invented details that relate to the conflicts.

If I were writing that Historical Military yarn, now would be the time to nail down the specific era and campaign, and put characters into different branches of the military. That Office Romance of yours now needs an industry, a time and a place.

Notes and Pointers

It's worth pointing out that this last diagram is (probably) a workable novel, but perhaps the hardest to understand. That's because it's the tip of the iceberg. The rest of the story is sitting in my head. So if you find *my* diagram of *my* novel confusing, that's fine. I'd be equally confused by yours! These tools are to help the writer. The only person who needs to understand your Conflict Diagram (or whatever) is *you*.

Some pointers to close on:

o **Not all conflicts get resolved:** Some conflicts—call them *tensions*—form part of the story world. For example, your series of books may have an ongoing romantic tension between the two protagonists, or the hero and villain may clash again and again, book after book... Mulder and Scully, Holmes and Moriaty.

o **All important conflicts lead back to the protagonist(s):** Otherwise—*duh!*—you have the wrong protagonist. (Or is your viewpoint character really a narrator, as per *The Great Gatsby*, or there to unearth other people's stories, as per the Detective genre?)

o **When personifying forces, one force per character:** This not only keeps things simple, it also nicely populates your story world. Avoid creating a Ms Rabbit from the *Peppa Pig* cartoons, who is a minor character but fills several roles. The exception, of course, is that the characters you want to focus on can be as complex as you like.

o **The diagram doesn't tell the story:** That's what the other tools are for! Read on!

But first, try it out!

Conflict Diagram Exercises

Using the diagramming tool of your choice, build the conflicts for the following in the genre(s) of your choice:
o **Start with a character:** Plunge a character into a vague situation. Use a Conflict Diagram to explore their story, discovering friends and enemies, and the various forces at work.
o **Start with a milieu:** Use a Conflict Diagram to invent or explore a milieu and the various forces at work within it. Then personify the forces, discover a protagonist and explore their story.
o **Start with a story:** Take a story you have in your head, or know well, and interrogate it to discover the conflicts using a Conflict Diagram.

Story Outline

My Story Outline is pretty much what you'd expect, but written in a style specifically intended to make it *writable*. Its immediate purpose is to let me evolve a story that feels right. Its ultimate purpose is to be hacked up into a Chapter Outline (see below, "**Chapter Outline**") telling me what to put in each chapter. (However, I have to grow it before it can do that, which usually means cycling through the Story Sculpting tools a few times. Once I have a rough Story Outline, the next step is usually to use Story QABNs to find the shape of the story, and then revisit the Story Outline again.)

Outlines: You're doing it wrong

Typically, a novice writer (*me, several years back!*) tries an outline perhaps once, finds it doesn't help, then gives up on the approach. This is probably because the failed outline reads like this:

```
King dies in battle against usurpers.
Princess flees.
Princess travels across the Wastelands of Doom.
Princess meets wizard who tests her.
Princess passes test.
Princess settles into new life as apprentice wizard.
```

That *could* be a summary of a damn good Fantasy novel. However, on its own, it's not very useful for writing the novel because it's just a shopping list, or perhaps an itinerary describing completed actions. There's no game-like rhythm of move and countermove.

As we'll see, it's not a bad first jotting if the writer were working towards building a proper outline. Typically, though, a novice will simply sit down with, say, "Princess flees", try draft a chapter by milking the melodrama, then run out of steam.

How then do you expand the original itinerary into a proper Story Outline?

How to write a writable Story Outline

It's easiest to write a Story Outline if you already have the story's conflicts (see above, **"Conflict Diagram"** on page 19) in mind. You can use your storyteller instinct to let the characters play out their various struggles while discovering things about your story world. However, it could be that you have an intuitive sense of some of these, and prefer to discover the rest. Perhaps you have a cool opening and want to see where it leads. Or perhaps what really matters is that itinerary: you want to take the Princess from battlefield, to wastelands, to wizard's tower, but need a story to bring it to life. It's certainly true that it's better to discover through building an Outline on the fly than through drafting text. If you hit a dead end with an Outline, you can just tweak a few paragraphs. With a draft, you lose hours of lovingly crafted prose!

My Outlines are woven out of chains of what I think of as *moves* and countermoves in one or more conflicts, pretty much like the transcription of a game of chess. I do this using natural language:

> The Enemy kills the King in battle, but the Princess finds the inner strength to escape. Alas, her path leads her to the Wasteland of Doom...

If we use brackets to break this up into moves we get:

> [The Enemy kill the King in battle], but [the Princess finds the inner strength to escape]. Alas, [her path leads her to the Wasteland of Doom...]

You'll immediately notice that all moves are linked by the word "but" or one of its many near-synonyms that imply some kind of reversal or complication. In fact, just using the word "but" is a good discipline, though it creates rather breathless prose:

> The enemy kills the King in battle, but the Princess finds the inner strength to escape, but her path leads her to the Wasteland of Doom, but...

So a writable Story Outline is a chain of moves strung together with buts, even if you can't see them. (A bit like that Yoko Ono and Andy Warhol film with nothing but people's rear ends, the more buts the better!) This gives us a rule of the thumb for testing the structure: *No buts, no novel.*

Sometimes you also need a "But elsewhere" or "But meanwhile" to show stuff going on in other locations. Just after the Princess flees the battle:

> But back at the Castle, the Evil Usurper gathers his minions and sends them after the Princess.

Note I said "*But___.*" It's usually not good enough to skip to a different location and show events that will *eventually* impact on the story. It just feels wrong:

> Meanwhile, an Elf Maiden proposes to her True Love, but is rejected.

Rather, it's best to have some kind of conflict, or clash, between each adjacent move. This can be as direct as the Evil Usurper planning a Princess hunt (above), or something more subtle like:

> But meanwhile, in the tranquillity of the Deep Forest, an Elf Maiden proposes to her True Love, but is rejected.

Perhaps it's enough that the forest *really* contrasts with the mayhem of the battlefield so much so that there is a kind of conflict of mood or aesthetics. Done right, you can also get away with things like, "But, weirdly, meanwhile...", and "But, mysteriously." (As usual, the test here is: when you imagine reading this, does it feel right?)

There's something else missing. What ties this to "*The Princess flees into the Wasteland of Doom*"? It's looking suspiciously like we've broken the Elf Maiden's heart just to provide a little helper for the Princess. That makes me feel a bit guilty. How about instead:

> But meanwhile, in the tranquillity of the Deep Forest, an Elf Maiden proposes to her True Love, but is rejected. She vows to use Dark Magic to win him back. For this she will need the heart of a human maiden.

Aha! Now the Princess is in trouble!

(Though it's not how I write, some authors build a plot out of mostly physically disconnected single moves: *"Man #1 arrives at airport. In a different city, Man 2 meets a Mafia don."* Each move is written as a vignette or short story and the overall effect depends on the genre. A Thriller writer, for example, may be playing with reader anticipation and curiosity. For a more Literary writer, the short stories and vignettes may themselves be the point.)

Expanding your Story Outline

The trick is to get it to the point where it reads like a real story. It helps if you avoid passive English and always have somebody *doing* their verb to someone else. This is more immediately engaging—just one of those general rules of the thumb—and you want your outline to engage your imagination. It also forces you to populate your story with characters who may in turn feed your imagination.

For example, I had "…but is rejected". It's better to have "but he rejects her".

And so the Story Outline expands.

```
The King fights the usurper, but the
usurper slays him and routs his army. The
Princess finds the inner strength to
escape towards the Wasteland of Doom.

But meanwhile in the tranquillity of the
Deep Forest, an Elf Maiden proposes to her
True Love, but he rejects her. She vows to
use Dark Magic to win him back. For this
she will need the heart of a human maiden.
She sets off towards the Wasteland of
Doom.

Worse still(!), the Evil Usurper gathers
his minions and sends them after the
Princess.
```

Visualise, try to… *remember* your novel as it evolves, getting closer and closer until you are either stuck, or else have something that feels right. Try to make everything hang together, avoid logical "plot holes", but don't worry too much. You're not done yet.

Climax and Ending

Now it's time to consider the Climax and the Ending, even if you haven't discovered them yet.

The **Climax** is the big happening near the end of your novel. It's the Chapel Perilous, the Hall of Testing, the *Battle Royale*. It's the place where the main characters succeed or fail, live or die. It's where the main conflicts resolve (whether or not you have diagrammed them).

> Evil Lord's men trap the Princess, but she finds the inner strength to leap into the marsh and they write her off as dead. However, the Elf Maiden is not fooled and follows.
>
> The Elf Maiden catches up with the Princess and easily overpowers her. However, the Princess refuses to give up and uses her courtly skills to make the Elf Maiden break down; what worth is love if it is constrained by magic? The Elf Maiden attempts suicide, but the Princess saves her. By ancient elvish custom, the Elf Maiden is now the slave of the Princess.

Um, yes.

You're thinking, *What happened to the Wizard?*

The thing is, he hasn't really featured in the story so far. He's just an objective, what I called a Bone of Contention (see "**Bone of Contention**" on page 19); no more a player in the story than "The Sea" or "Peace on Earth". The Climax has to be some kind of fight—literal or otherwise—between the different players or it just won't feel like a climax.

The Climax is almost always the biggest event depicted near the end of your novel. If you show your characters fighting at the Battle of Waterloo, for example, and that takes place towards the end of your novel, then that's your climax, not the emotional confrontation in the aftermath. A ginormous military action simply has too much gravitas to be upstaged by men crying on each other.

If, however, the emotional confrontation really matters to you and the battle really doesn't, either skip the battle and show the aftermath, or—better!—use the battle to equip the characters for the confrontation.

In other words, the Climax should set up…

The **Ending** is the bit where the dust settles from the Climax, we see the results and people announce decisions they made during or because of the Climax: "Having faced death in battle against the French, I am now ready to face up to my own homosexuality. Kiss me, Marshal Blücher." And so on.

```
Together the Princess and the Elf stagger
up to the door of the Wizard's tower. The
Princess knocks and the door swings open…

Together they will face the Wizard. What
happens next? Coming soon, Book Two in the
Princess and Elf Trilogy: "Freudian
Landmark of the Jungian Archetype"!
```

It's possible that your Ending *feels* right to you. Equally, your storyteller instinct may be screaming that you need a better Ending. However, first you need to consider your Story QABNs, for which see the next chapter ("**Story QABNs**" on page 41).

Worldbuilding and the Story Outline

Writing the Story Outline usually involves doing some worldbuilding as you identify things such as specific props and locations.

You still don't need to go into detail at this stage. For example, I don't need to know the order of battle of the King's army; if I need a map, it's only a rough one, and I don't need to know the layout of the location for that final confrontation. Similarly, if my Military Historical takes me to a tavern, I don't yet need to know what, say, an 18th century Spanish tavern is like. Your Office Romance, however, needs some interior locations, for example Copy Room, Canteen, Meeting Room, Open Plan Office. Don't feel the need to pick a colour scheme, though!

There are three reasons for delaying going into detail. First, detailed worldbuilding is a different kind of activity from writing, and switching between activities will have a time overhead since each time you do it will take about fifteen minutes to get back "into the zone". Second, you may end up over-researching and spending time, say, on the History of Taverns, rather than writing. Third and last, you may subsequently decide to bin that section of the novel and your research will have been wasted!

Story Outline Exercises

Using "but", "however", "worse", etc constructions, see how far you get writing an outline for the following:
o An idea that just popped into your head.
o One of the conflict diagrams you produced in the previous exercise.
O Middle-aged divorcee goes to sleepy fishing village to find herself, only to face a zombie attack.

Story QABNs

Are you old enough to remember when the BBC punted out the 1930s *Buck Rogers* series on Saturday Morning TV? "*Is our hero really dead? Tune in next week...*" You see this all the time at the end of the modern season finales, for instance *Castle*: *"Will Becket [SPOILER DELETED]? Tune in next season!"*

Crude but effective.

It is, after all, the kind of tense curiosity we generally call "suspense" that keeps people interested in a story. In other words, the story poses questions and answers them in interesting ways. I do this more formally, using what I called the QABN to give shape to the different parts of my story and tie it all together.

I tend to look at Story QABNs once I have a rough Story Outline (see above, **"Story Outline"** on page 34). However, if your story is focussed on relationships between characters, you may want to go straight from Conflicts to QABNs, and then to Outline. Finally, if you are most interested in the challenges facing a character, you may want to start with Story QABNs and then try the Story Outline.

Introducing the QABN (pronounced "Cabin")

I think that the most interesting story questions are about characters in conflict:

```
Can the hero defeat the bad guy and marry
the handsome prince?
```

However, I like novels where people blow shit up and have swordfights! It's possible that your reading is driven by less bellicose questions relating to the story world and its people:

```
Who killed the Reverend Plum?

Will the Elves really leave?
```

Interesting questions usually have interesting answers:

```
Can the hero defeat the bad guy and marry
the handsome prince? Yes, but she chooses
to remain single.

Who killed the Reverend Plum? His
```

> housekeeper, but because he took advantage of her unrequited love for him.
>
> *Will the Elves really leave?* No, but they turn out to be so evil people wish they had.

Answers are the most interesting when they have implications:

> *Can the hero defeat the bad guy and marry the handsome prince?* Yes, but she chooses to remain single. Now she must find her self-esteem in other ways.
>
> *Who killed the Reverend Plum?* His housekeeper, but because he took advantage of her unrequited love for him. Now his life is revealed as one of hypocrisy.
>
> *Will the Elves really leave?* No, but they turn out to be so evil people wish they had. Now humanity must fight a long war to expel them.

All this leads me to a boilerplate form—not quite, I hope, a formula—for this:

[Question] [Answer] [But...] [Now...]

I call this the QABN (pronounced "Cabin", though feel free to give it a more Fantasy pronunciation, if you please, e.g. "*!K Ab'n*").

A QABN can sound very like a modified "elevator pitch" for an entire story:

> *When Ninjas abduct the werewolf hero's human girlfriend, can he overcome his fear of heights in order to rescue her?* Yes, but in doing so he realises she is not a worthy mate. Now he must travel to the Russian Steppes in search of love.

The QABN is most useful to help reveal the components of

the story:

> *Can the werewolf hero beat the Ninjas in hand-to-hand combat?* Yes, but they use the girl as bait and capture him in a silver net. Now he must escape certain doom!

A good QABN usually relates to a conflict or struggle, a powerful clash of ideas, or an intriguing mystery. However, you should be able to tell if it's any good simply by reading it aloud and trusting your instincts.

Using Story QABNs to understand your story

The main use of the Story QABN is to capture the shape of your story. The trick is to list *all* the interesting QABNs relating to your protagonist. If you've prepared a good Conflicts Diagram or Story Outline, then most of these questions will have another character at the other end of them. If you're actually starting with Story QABNs, that's fine; just make stuff up (it's what we do!) and tinker with them later.

Here's some Story QABNs for *The Princess and the Elf Maiden* (see **"Outlines: You're doing it wrong"** on page 34). I've written them down as they came to me, without editing or revising:

> *Can the Princess escape the Legions of the Evil Usurper?* Yes, by faking her own death. However, the Elf Maiden follows her. Now they must fight.
>
> *Can the Princess escape the Elf Maiden (who wants to use her heart in a black magic love spell?)* No. Now they must fight.
>
> *Can the Princess beat the Elf Maiden in hand-to-hand combat?* Oddly, no. However, she uses psychology to destroy her. Now she must save her from suicide.

> *Can the Princess save the Elf Maiden from suicide?* Yes, but only because of the inner strength gained from the whole chase experience. Now the Elf must obey her.
>
> *Can the King defeat the Usurper?* No, but he dies making time for his sister to escape. Now she must find the inner strength to get to the Tower of the Wizard.
>
> *Can the Princess make it to the Tower of the Wizard?* Yes, but only by discovering her Inner Strength. Now she doesn't need the wizard and will return to take on the usurper herself! However, the Wizard opts to come with her since she has proven herself worthy.

Whoa! Did *I* write that last one? I love that idea. OK. That means I can also add this one:

> *Can the Princess, with help from the Elf, reach the tower?* Yes, but the Princess decides to return to restore her dynasty. Now the next book will be considerably more violent than this one.

Once you've got this list, it's time to sort them into structural categories. It's easier *not* to do this in chronological order. Don't be afraid to tweak the questions to fit—that's the point of this tool.

First, go through and pick out all those QABNs that just describe the very **Start** of the story, the incidents that kick off the adventure but don't feature throughout it:

> *Can the King defeat the Usurper?* No, but he dies making time for his sister to escape. Now she must find the inner strength to get to the Tower of the Wizard.

Now look for the **Climax,** the big set-piece scene near the end of the novel (see "**Climax and Ending**" on page 39):

> *Can the Princess beat the Elf Maiden in hand-to-hand combat? Oddly, no. However, she uses psychology to destroy her. Now she must save her from suicide.*
>
> *Can the Princess save the Elf Maiden from suicide? Yes, but only because of the inner strength gained from the whole chase experience. Now the Elf must obey her.*

Now find the QABNs that connect the two, the **Setup**:

> *Can the Princess escape the Legions of the Evil Usurper? Yes, by faking her own death. However, the Elf Maiden follows her. Now they must fight.*
>
> *Can the Princess escape the Elf Maiden (who wants to use her heart in a black magic love spell?) No. Now they must fight.*

Now pull out the ones relating to *only* the **Ending**:

> *Can the Princess, with help from the Elf, reach the tower? Yes, but the Princess decides to return to restore her dynasty. Now the next book will be considerably more violent than this one.*

Presented in chronological order left to right, we get a table like this:

Start	Setup	Climax	Ending
Can the King defeat the Usurper? No, but he dies making time for his sister to escape. Now she must find the inner strength to get to the Tower of the Wizard.	Can the Princess escape the Legions of the Evil Usurper? Yes, by faking her own death. However, the Elf Maiden follows her. Now they must fight. Can the Princess escape the Elf Maiden (who wants her heart for a black magic love spell?) No. Now they must fight.	Can the Princess beat the Elf Maiden in hand-to-hand combat? No. However, she uses psychology to destroy her. Now she must save her from suicide. Can the Princess save the Elf Maiden from suicide? Yes, but only because of the inner strength gained from the whole chase experience. Now the Elf must obey her.	Can the Princess, with help from the Elf, reach the tower? Yes, but the Princess decides to return to restore her dynasty. Now the next book will be considerably more violent than this one.

We now need some QABNs to tie the story together.

First, grab the one that describes the **Whole Story**, in effect bracketing the Setup, Climax and Ending. This is likely to be touchy-feely or thematic:

```
Can the Princess make it to the Tower of
the Wizard? Yes, but only by discovering
her Inner Strength. Now she doesn't need
the wizard and will return to take on the
usurper herself! However, the Wizard opts
to come with her since she has proved
herself worthy.
```

Then plug in another QABN for the **Good Bits**, the Setup and Climax... Whoops! I don't have that one. That's OK, I can make one up:

```
Can the Princess physically defeat the Elf
Maiden? No, but ironically, surviving the
Elf Maiden's chase gives her the strength
to mentally defeat the Elf Maiden. Now
```

```
together they will face the Tower of the
Wizard.
```

Using the Table of Doom to tighten the structure of your Story Outline

At this point, I usually feel the need to tabulate the whole thing. I call this the Table of Doom (because, *writer!*):

Start	Setup	Climax	Ending
Can the King defeat the Usurper? No, but he dies making time for his sister to escape. Now she must find the inner strength to get to the Tower of the Wizard.	Can the Princess escape the Legions of the Evil Usurper? Yes, by faking her own death. However, the Elf Maiden follows her. Now they must fight. Can the Princess escape the Elf Maiden (who wants to use her heart in a black magic love spell?) No. Now they must fight.	Can the Princess beat the Elf Maiden in hand-to-hand combat? No. However, she uses psychology to destroy her. Now she must save her from suicide. Can the Princess save the Elf Maiden from suicide? Yes, but only because of the inner strength gained from the whole chase experience. Now the Elf must obey her.	Can the Princess, with help from the Elf, reach the tower? Yes, but the Princess decides to return to restore her dynasty. Now the next book will be considerably more violent than this one.
	Good Bits: Can the Princess physically defeat the Elf Maiden? No, but ironically, surviving the Elf Maiden's chase gives her the strength to mentally defeat the Elf Maiden. Now together they will face the Tower of the Wizard.		
Whole Story: Can the Princess make it to the Tower of the Wizard? Yes, but only by discovering her Inner Strength. Now she doesn't need the wizard and will return to take on the usurper herself! However, the Wizard opts to come with her since she is worthy.			

(I usually use spreadsheet software to do this; however, most word processing programs support tables like this, and you can always use a scrap of paper and pencils (or a charred mammoth bone and a cave wall, you Luddite!))

The Table of Doom is not just a way of explaining how the story works, it *is* the story viewed from one perspective. It lets us see how everything fits, look for patterns and connections, and then use our storyteller instinct to improve the greater whole.

Let's quickly revisit the structural elements:

o The **Start** contains what are sometimes called the "inciting incidents". All that really matters is that when we meet them, the characters are already in conflict with something, and that the result kicks off the story by motivating the characters to take action.

o The **Setup** contains most of your story's word count and is what people often call the "middle". I prefer my term because it conveys the purpose of this part of the story, which is to set up the Climax. It does this by (i) equipping the characters for the climax, and (ii) building the big conflict resolved in the climax.

o The **Climax** is the big clash at the end, where ninjas explode and rockets fly and stuff like that. The Climax needs to logically follow the Setup.

o The **Ending** is where the chickens come home to roost.

Now, considering my Table of Doom, I notice that some form of inner strength is a recurring theme and I am drawn to a more literary **Thematic Question**.

The end result of tinkering is this:

Start	Setup	Climax	Ending
Can the King defeat the Usurper? No, but he dies making time for his sister to escape. Now she must find the Inner Strength to get to the Tower of the Wizard.	Can the Princess escape the Legions of the Evil Usurper? Yes, by finding her Inner Strength and ultimately faking her own death. However, the Elf Maiden follows her. Now they must fight.	Can the Princess beat the Elf Maiden in hand-to-hand combat? No. However, her Inner Strength enables her to keep going and use psychology to destroy her. Now she must save her from suicide.	Can the Princess, with help from the Elf, reach the tower? Yes, but equipped with her Inner Strength the Princess decides to return to restore her dynasty. Now the next book will be considerably more violent than this one.
	Can the Princess escape the Elf Maiden (who wants to use her heart in a black magic love spell?) No, however the chase gives her her Inner Strength. Now they must fight.	Can the Princess save the Elf Maiden from suicide? Yes, but only because of the Inner Strength gained from the whole chase experience. Now the Elf must obey her.	
	Can the Princess physically defeat the Elf Maiden? No, but ironically, surviving the Elf Maiden's chase gives her the Inner Strength to mentally defeat the Elf Maiden. Now together they will face the Tower of the Wizard.		
Can the Princess make it to the Tower of the Wizard? Yes, but only by discovering her Inner Strength. Now she doesn't need the wizard and will return to take on the usurper herself! However, the Wizard opts to come with her since she is worthy.			
THEME: Can a Princess (i.e. educated, civilised young woman) be tough? Yes, intellectual ability can translate into Inner Strength.			

Armed with a table like this, you are now ready to tackle your Story Outline, either writing it from scratch or tinkering with what you have. You can also revisit your Conflict Diagram; however, there is no need for this if you feel you can write from the Table of Doom.

Using Story QABNs as a way in

If you are more interested in a character's journey than in the opposition they face, then you may find Story QABNs are actually the best way into a novel. Let's try it for something literary:

> Can Angsty Artist find himself? Yes, but only when he mans up and gets involved in the world. Now he must adapt to his new self-knowledge.

So far so good. But it needs to be more specific! What situation does he get himself into?

> Can Angsty Artist escape to South America to find himself? Yes, but drug-funded guerrillas attack his village. Now he must help with the defence…

Oooh! Oh, damn! I said I would be more literary. LitFic tends to like deprived working-class settings at times of social unrest with a soft left bias. How about this as a **Start**:

> Can Arty escape to a cheap studio in a Yorkshire mill town in order to find himself? Yes, but the 1980s industrial unrest disrupts the local population. Now he must avoid getting involved.

OK. Beards, miner's hats, social class and privilege. I can feel my first Booker Prize coming on. However, his situation seems too easy, not messy enough. How about:

> When Arty gets an Arts Council grant to record working class life in a Yorkshire mill town, can he use the expected solitude in order to "find himself"? Yes, but the local factory is laying off half its employees, triggering strikes and

riots. Now he must avoid getting involved.

Better. Now we need a **Setup**. The trick is to grab the "Now…" clause from the previous QABN plus any context:

> Can Arty sketch the workers and their families without getting involved? Yes, but the authenticity of working-class experience ultimately shames him. Now he must help.

I've no idea how he could help—we don't have enough context yet! That's OK, we'll find it eventually. So the **Climax** needs to be something like:

> Can Arty use his art to help the strikers? No, the spin doctors of the evil bosses have the media sewn up. However, his camera footage enables him to reveal the brutality of the hired security goons. Now he must…WHAT?

Now he must what? I think this is a redemptive moment, so suppose:

> Can Arty use his art to help the Strikers? No, the spin doctors of the evil bosses have the media sewn up. However, his camera footage enables him to reveal the brutality of the hired security goons. Now he must eat humble pie and hand it over to the Local Activist.

Interesting, now we finally have another character on the scene. Suppose Lenny the Local Activist is Arty's antagonist. Lenny thinks Art is a sideshow and that only practical things matter in the current situation. Oh, and let's have a bit of homoerotic tension between arty Arty and macho Lenny. (I want my literary prize.)

So now we backtrack to the Setup:

> Can Arty convince Lenny that his Art

project matters? No, the Strikers' situation is too grim and ultimately they fall out. However, Arty feels validated by 1930s Socialist Art and decides to help. Now he must use his art to win the PR battle!

This gives us the Ending:

Can Arty give the footage to Lenny? Yes, but Lenny has Arty's art strewn around the walls of his office, and is clearly overawed by it. Validation for Arty! The pair become lovers. Now Arty has found himself and must stay to help the town.

Let's put Arty and Lenny into the Table of Doom:

Start	Setup	Climax	Ending
When Arty gets an Arts Council grant to record working class life in a Yorkshire mill town, can he use the expected solitude in order to "find himself"? Yes, but the local factory is laying off half its employees, triggering strikes and riots. Now he must avoid getting involved.	Can Arty sketch the workers and their families without getting involved? Yes, but the authenticity of working class experience ultimately shames him. Now he must help. Can Arty convince Lenny that his Art project matters? No, the Strikers' situation is too grim and ultimately they fall out. However, Arty feels validated by 1930s Socialist Art and decides to help. Now he must use his art to win the PR battle!	Can Arty use his art to help the Strikers? No, the spin doctors of the evil bosses have the media sewn up. However, his camera footage enables him to reveal the brutality of the hire security goons. Now he must eat humble pie and hand it over to the Lenny.	Can Arty give the footage to Lenny? Yes, but Lenny has Arty's art strewn around the walls of his office, and is clearly overawed by it. Validation for Arty! The pair become lovers. Now Arty has found himself and must stay to help the town.
	Can Arty prove that Art matters in the real world? No. However, he himself as a person can make a difference. Now he must eat humble pie and hand over his film to Lenny.		
Can Angsty Artist find himself? Yes but only when he mans up and gets involved in the world. Now he must adapt to his new self-knowledge. THEME: Is Art relevant? Yes, but only in its place. Now we must all embrace practical political activism.			

You'll note that I found a new QABN for the meat of the story, and also identified an interesting thematic one. Armed with this table, I'm ready to create an Outline for this story. Unfortunately, I have to wash my hair first.

Story QABN Exercises

Using the QABN construction ("Question... Answer... But... Now...") try the following:

o Take Arty and Lenny's Table of Doom and tweak a few of the questions to change the political and moral viewpoint, e.g. making it Ayn Randian, Libertarian, Social Conservative, Radical Feminist, Magical Realist or Surrealist.
o Jot down some QABNs for a random idea that popped into your head and fight them into a Table of Doom.
O Take an outline from the previous exercise (see "**Story Outline Exercises**"); create QABNs and then a Table of Doom.

Barbarian in the City

By now you will have started to agree with me: there's no right way in. Just because there's a logical order for presenting these tools, doesn't mean that your creative process needs to follow that order.

Though this seems time-consuming, by working at this level we're weaving and potentially unraveling mere hundreds of words. A "discovery writer" who is "pantsing" is hazarding tens of thousands of words and risking getting lost in the text whenever they have to deal with structural issues. To give you an idea of this blurry, messy process, let's go back to *Barbarian in the City*.

First stab at the outline for *Barbarian in the City*

You'll remember the Conflict Diagram looked a bit like this:

M Harold Page
BARBARIAN IN THE CITY

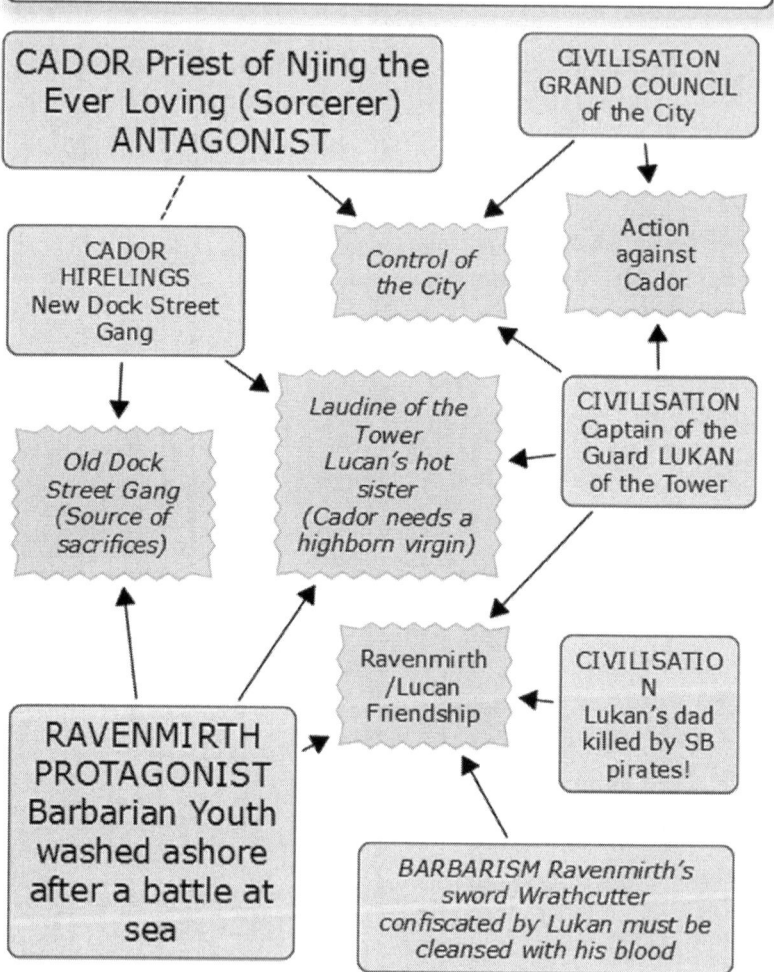

My first stab at an outline produces:

> A storm tide washes Ravenmirth ashore. The street gangs fight over the right to loot his body for the sword WRATHCUTTER, but he

> regains consciousness and drives off the evil New Dock Gang, killing several of them.

What happens next? Just looking at that conflict diagram, I have a sense of how the characters play their game:

> The Old Dockers had planned to rob Ravenmirth, but instead welcome him to their den. When he sleeps, OD Leader 1 wants to murder and rob him but OD Leader 2 argues not. OD1 slays OD2 and proceeds with plan. However, Ravenmirth wakes and kills him. The surviving gang members are afraid of either being slain, or else expiring due to lack of protection. But Ravenmirth, impelled by his barbarian code, declares himself their king.

(At this point, I realise I probably need a Conflict Diagram for the gang itself and I need to start populating the Cast List. However, I'm going to keep going for now and see what I discover.)

> Meanwhile, the depleted New Dockers limp back to their squat. NEW DOCKER LEADER is getting too old for this and realises he hardly knows his gang any more. Worse, up and coming RIVAL GANG 3, emboldened by the New Docker defeat, arrives to evict them. However, CADOR THE PRIEST OF NJING appears and drives them off with impressive mojo. He offers the New Dockers money and magic items in return for kidnapping younger street people and delivering them to the temple. The New Dockers agree and want to strike against the Old Dockers. New Docker Leader agrees. However, he's more interested in career development and directs them to easy targets first…

> CAPTAIN LUKAN oversees the policing of the Docks. (He could pay a deputy to do this, but doesn't want anybody taking bribes.) The son of a respectable trader has been kidnapped. Lukan plays detective and finds street kids have also gone missing...but nobody wants to talk about it. However, he hears about the newly-strong Old Docker gang and decides to visit.
>
> Meanwhile, Ravenmirth has driven off local rival gangs, enabling the Old Dockers to hang onto their pilfering, and stop paying protection money when they do legitimate jobs. He has also started drilling his gang in basic martial arts. At a barbarian-style feast, Ravenmirth frets because he craves a more heroic victory. SIDEKICK is mildly terrified and does his best to persuade him against anything rash. At this point, enter Captain Lukan.

Oooh! I'm liking this. Ravenmirth treats the city as any other location and makes like a barbarian king. I have a whole jumble of visions from this, but there's no need to write them down. They'll be there when I need them.

> Ravenmirth did have sentries, etc., but they never resist the Town Guard. Captain Lukan is amused by the feast, but demands the sword Wrathcutter (swords are illegal for commoners). Ravenmirth wants to fight him, Lukan is reminded of his slain father and tempted, but Sidekick persuades Ravenmirth to avoid a massacre and give up the sword...for now. The guardsmen want to slaughter the gang, but Lukan says they have done no crime, and finding no clues to the kidnappings, exits.
>
> Lukan returns home to the Tower; a

crumbling castle now absorbed by the city's suburbs. He bitches about work to his sister LAUDINE, who says, well, obviously, the victims end up in the Temple of Njing; she has a good view of the compound's back door from her bedroom window. Lukan resolves to lie in wait.

(Good thing I never drew a map of the city!)

That night, impelled by honour, Ravenmirth comes to the Tower for his sword. Sidekick acts as guide, but does not come in. Ravenmirth feels guilty about potentially leaving his people in the lurch, but honour is honour; he must retrieve his sword. Expecting heavy guards, he breaks into the house via a high window and surprises Laudine in her chamber…

Captain Lukan (plus his Guards) lies in wait at the temple back door. The New Dockers arrive with victims. However, they use canned mojo in order to get past Lukan and his guards. Lukan resolves to raid the temple in the morning, "when magic is at its weakest". He picks up a NECKLACE dropped by one of the prisoners. [I had to dive back and put that in.]

Meanwhile, Laudine is using her poise and charm to handle Ravenmirth. She plans to just give him his sword back and send him on his way. However, he imprisons her and waits to fight her brother; don't worry, it will be a fair fight.

Lukan comes home to find Ravenmirth waiting. He accuses Ravenmirth of hurting Laudine, but R shows him L is safe and demands to fight. Lukan, who is busy,

```
offers him 24 hours to get out of town
instead, and promises the Old Dockers are
safe. R thanks him but still wants to
fight. They fight to a standstill. R
notices the necklace [had to go back and
put that in!]—it comes from an Old Docker!
He accuses Lukan of having already fallen
on his friends. Lukan explains about the
temple. Ravenmirth immediately offers to
help him.
…ARGH!
```

Now I am stuck. It's time to look at the Story QABNs.

Story QABNs for *Barbarian in the City*

So, staring at my outline so far, and tinkering, I end up with this Table of Doom:

	Start	Setup	Climax	Ending
	Can RAVENMIRTH survive his arrival in the City? Yes but he ends up controlling the Old Dockers gang. Now he must play barbarian chief.	Can the barbarian RAVENMIRTH get his sword back from Lukan and then slay him? Yes, but CADOR has kidnapped his people. Now he must postpone revenge in order to help Lukan.	Can Lukan and Ravenmirth break into the temple and rescue their people? Yes, but only by adopting each other's virtues. Now they must reach an accommodation.	Can Lukan and Ravenmirth reach an accommodation? Yes, at Laudine's suggestion… (1) They become blood brothers, thus negating the feud. (2) Lukan arranges for the Ravenmirth to own the property in which his gang squats. However, Cador's patrons in the Grand Council plot revenge on both of them! Tune in next week…
		Can the civilised LUKAN investigate CADOR's temple legitimately? No, the Grand Council block him. Worse, Cador abducts Laudine. Now Lukan must accept help from the barbarian.		
		Can Ravenmirth slay Lukan? No way of knowing. Adventure bonds them. Now they must reach an accommodation.		
THEME: Which is better, barbarism or civilisation? Neither. Humanity needs both sets of values in order to thrive.				

First, note that not all these questions would make any sense unless you had already read the first stab at the outline.

Now let's tinker.

Tinkering with the Story Outline and the Story QABNs

The first thing I'm seeing is that this feels more like a Conan novella than a 100K word doorstop. I'm not worried. I'll find more story as I write. If not, I'll treat this as the first third of a longer novel, plugging the Ending of this table into the Start of the next one.

Next, I notice that Lukan and Ravenmirth need to hit the temple *at the same time*. This gives me a good conclusion to that duel scene:

> Lukan comes home to find Ravenmirth waiting. He accuses Ravenmirth of hurting Laudine, but R shows him L is safe and demands to fight. Lukan, who is busy, offers him 24 hours to get out of town instead, and promises the Old Dockers are safe. R thanks him but still wants to fight. They fight to a standstill. R notices the necklace—it comes from an Old Docker! He accuses Lukan of having already fallen on his friends. Lukan explains about the temple. Ravenmirth immediately offers to help him. However, Laudine has escaped and summoned help. Ravenmirth ends up in the city jail.

...Great! I can show Ravenmirth trying to escape and Lukan trying to go through channels. I like the implicit parallel between jail and bureaucracy.

There's also the issue of the Climax seeming a bit low-budget. I'll need to think of ways to pimp it up a bit. I like my casts of thousands. Perhaps Cador is using human sacrifice to assemble a mighty skeleton army, and we can have mob versus skeletons mass action?

Finally, the theme of Barbarism vs Civilisation seems a little crass. I suspect that as I write, this will refine. For a start, both Lukan and Ravenmirth are actually bound by their own sets of rules...perhaps the adventure teaches them about their shared values. We'll see.

Now it's time for me to return to the Story Outline. Once I've got the Ending, I'll make any changes that come to me, especially dropping in things to support a big fight at the end. For example, let's have the Temple of Njing the All-Loving serve as the military cemetery, thus giving Cador a nice source of warrior skeletons, and also the possibility of Lukan facing the skeleton of his own father. Perhaps we can meet Lukan for the first time as he investigates the tampering with the graves of war heroes?

Then, at last, I'll start Drafting, which is where we're going now... after this exercise, that is.

Story Sculpting Tools: Summary

o Use the three tools in any order, and jump between them as required.
o Use the Conflict Diagram to find the interesting conflicts. Do this by noting Players, Bones of Contention, and the connections between them.
o Use the Story Outline to capture the pub or coffee shop narrative. It should read like a story and use the word "but" a lot.
o Use the Story QABNs (Question-Answer-But-Now) to nail the shape of the story, namely Start, Setup, Climax and Ending.
O Test everything against your storyteller instinct.

Story Sculpting Tools: Exercises

Using Conflict Diagrams and Story QABNs, generate a complete Story Outline for one or more of the following:
o One of the stories you created in an earlier exercise.
o A Romance between a secret Ninja and a lonely Statistician.
o A Revenge Western in Space with Ninjas and Dinosaurs.

5. STORYTELLING TOOLS

Story Sculpting	Storytelling
Conflict Diagrams	Chapter Outline
Story QABNs	Scene QABNs
Story Outlines	Scene Outlines
TEXT	

So you've got the Story Outline and it's time to start writing.

This is where I used to get stuck. How *do* you go from a few words in an outline to a fully-fledged scene?

I use three more tools, really just tweaked versions of the same ones I used during Story Sculpting. That's one reason why this chapter is shorter than the previous one. The other reason is that things get easier the closer to the actual text you get.

Let me show you…

Chapter Outline

The Chapter Outline is just a boiled-down version of your regular Story Outline (see above, "**Story Outline**" on page 34). Unlike the latter, it doesn't have to read well. You already know characters and setting, so now it's time to create a summary to help you write. In doing so, you get a feeling for what your novel will be like to read, and your storyteller instinct may drive you to make changes—some minor, some sweeping. You'll also discover new things about your story world.

How to write a Chapter Outline

Take a paragraph from my *Barbarian in the City*:

> Meanwhile, the depleted New Dockers limp back to their squat. NEW DOCKER LEADER is getting too old for this and realises he hardly knows his gang any more. Worse, up and coming RIVAL GANG 3, emboldened by the New Docker defeat, arrives to evict them. However, CADOR THE PRIEST OF NJING appears and drives them off with impressive mojo. He offers the New Dockers money and magic items in return for kidnapping younger street people and delivering them to the temple. The New Dockers agree and want to strike against the Old Dockers. New Docker Leader agrees. However, he's more interested in career development and directs them to easy targets first…

In the Chapter Outline this might read as:

> NDs go to ground, but RG comes to evict them. Cador saves NDs, hires them, and gives them magic items. NDs want to strike against ODs, but jaded leader wants to cultivate Cador and directs them to easy targets.

I'm lazy, however, and thus is just notes, so I use and "X" to break up the opposing Moves (for more on Moves, see above, **"How to write a writable Story Outline"** on page 35):

> ND go to ground x but RG comes to evict them x Cador saves ND. C hires ND, gives them magic items x NDs want to strike against ODs x jaded leader wants to cultivate Cador; directs them to easy targets.

How to tell if there is enough plot in your chapter

So take the following bit of outline from the previous section:

> ND go to ground x but RG comes to evict them x Cador saves ND. C hires ND, gives them magic items x NDs want to strike against ODs x jaded leader wants to cultivate Cador; directs them to easy targets.

Is that enough for a chapter? Could be several, actually, if the New Dockers were the focus. However, they are not, so *yes*, this is a chapter. There's no hard and fast rule for this, it depends on your genre and ultimately experience of your own writing style. However, I tend to use the following as a guide:

o **A chapter (a) must contain at least one *clash* between moves, and (b) the final move must create suspense.**

It's easiest to explain this with an example. Suppose we *did* want to get two chapters out of that section:

> ND go to ground x but RG comes to evict them.

> Cador saves ND. C hires ND, gives them magic items x NDs want to strike against ODs x jaded leader wants to cultivate Cador; directs them to easy targets.

As it stands this does not work! In the first chapter we presumably see the New Dockers limping home, only to get jumped by the Rival Gang. Lots of description, I suppose, but not much actual edge-of-your seat conflict. Just thinking about it makes me yawn. The second chapter only gets interesting when the jaded leader must persuade his followers to go for easy targets. Let's see if we can improve these chapters.

o **EXERCISE – Have a go yourself, then read on...**

Did you have a go? I bet you skipped. Go on, at least look at that first chapter and see if you can make that better…

Ready or not, here we go! The first chapter already creates *suspense*; i.e., *What will happen when the Rival Gang comes to evict the New Dockers?* Any move that triggers an *"OMG! Now what?"* in the characters and/or the readers has a similar effect. For example, "Heroes capture the bunker" creates suspense if we know that they will now have to hold it against a million mechanised elves.

Moves creating suspense don't always generate much word count. For example, they can be a sudden revelation like the Rival Gang already being in residence (above), or an unexpected event such as—as per Chandler's Law—a man bursting into the room with a gun.

However, what this chapter needs is a *clash* where move and countermove happen simultaneously and something results. This is where the analogy with chess breaks down because we're interested in what precisely happens when, say, the knight tries to take the pawn, and there's no guarantee that the knight will succeed. (Perhaps the pawn has a crossbow.)

So let's have somebody oppose that trip across town. It might be handy to bring on Lukan earlier in the story, and as soon as he's on the scene, the following jumps into my head:

```
Lukan tries to arrest them x ND evade and
get   home   x   RG   have   already   taken
possession!
```

Better? We don't need a rule of the thumb because we can almost see this play out. However, if we do apply the rule of the thumb we can see that it contains the requisite clash and reversal:

```
[CLASH: Lukan tries to arrest them x ND
evade and get home] x RG have already
taken possession! OMG! Now what will they
do?
```

Now, the second chapter felt wrong because the really cool stuff with the Evil Wizard was actually *less* interesting than an urban gang arguing. Let's find some more conflict:

```
Cador saves ND. C offers to hire ND x
members suspicious x seeing his own
advantage, jaded leader convinces them.
NDs want to strike against ODs x intent on
```

```
pleasing C, jaded leader directs them to
easy targets.
```

Adding some brackets:

```
Cador saves ND. [CLASH: C offers to hire
ND x members suspicious x seeing his own
advantage, jaded leader convinces them].
[CLASH: NDs want to strike against ODs x
intent on pleasing C, jaded leader directs
them to easy targets]. OMG! Now what will
happen to the Old Docker gang?
```

So now we have two clashes, one with Fantasy tropes, the other more mundane. We also have *another* conflict; jaded leader versus gang. The novel is growing and we haven't typed anything yet. (OMG! We're stuck at zero word count!)

Will these *really* be long enough to be chapters? A chase through a cityscape is going to be pretty description heavy, so I'm fine with the first one. However, note that the description will be of the snipers-in-the-belfries-kind (see the next bit about Worldbuilding). The second has lots of stuff happening, so that'll be OK too. If not, we'll fix it later!

So what you do now is break the Story Outline into rough chapters, then work over *at least* the first third to make sure they are proper chapters. It's probably not worth going further than that because—in case you hadn't guessed—the story will grow with the telling.

If you discover new conflicts you can add them to your Conflicts Diagram, or simply update your notes. There's no need to keep your Story Outline up to date. That's probably served its purpose since the characters and the cool moments are now firmly lodged in your head and the more bare-bones Chapter Outline is the easiest place to track continuity and itineraries.

Once you have a good chunk of viable Chapter Outline, you can consider Scene Questions (which we'll come to shortly).

Worldbuilding in the Chapter Outline

Muster the cast lists! Unleash the maps of yore!

Knock yourself out!

The Chapter Outline is where you sort out all the annoying stuff that will otherwise mess up your novel. If timings and travel are important, draw maps. If interiors matter, draw plans. Most importantly—as you go—draw up a cast list of people and places including any physical or personality tags you're going to use, e.g. "belfries," "long-haired", "angry".

However, bear in mind the "Snipers in the Belfries" *Rule*. (See, above, The "Snipers in the Belfries" Rule.) Tags for people and places should affect the story.

The best tags are two-edged swords that create some kind of standing conflict (much like the "Aspects" used in *Fate* and other similar roleplaying systems). "Belfries" is good because they provide cover for both sides in a military yarn, and perhaps both motivation and a Bone of Contention in that steamy tale of building restoration we thought of earlier. The same goes for characters. For example, replace "Angry" with "Class Warrior" and you have a soldier who is great in a fight against aristocratic cavalry, but a liability at the Grand Ball. Replace "Long-haired" with "Hippy" and you have a friend who is—perhaps—both sensitive *and* unreliable. This approach gives us more vivid minor characters, and also gets around tag fatigue in readers since the tags will manifest in varied ways.

Where you have groups, it's helpful to pick one as a spokesperson/NCO/leader, and share out any specialisms.

For example:

```
Soldiers: Corporal Smith (NCO, Tommy Gun),
Private Willis (tall, grenades), Private
Johnson (scared, sharpshooter)

Office colleagues: Bella (busty, ring
leader), Janice (blond flirt), Jocasta
(country look, snobby intern)
```

When in doubt, read books in your genre and see how it's done.

Chapter Outline Exercises

o Take an Outline you wrote for the outlining exercise (see above, "**Story Outline Exercises**" on page 41) and turn the first third into proper chapters.
o Take an outline you have knocking around and turn some of it into a Chapter Outline. (I bet you can't.)
o Imagine a small community or team and draw up a cast list.

Scene QABNs

So, now we have to get from Chapter Outline to scenes, and the way I do it is using Scene QABNs. You've already met my QABN construction, but let's see it again (because flicking back and forward is distracting):

o Question-Answer-But-Now...

The Scene QABN should make clear the conflict (who's trying to do what and what's stopping them), capture the focus for the writing scene, and nail any motivations. For example:

> Can Jocasta prepare dinner in time for the arrival of her in-laws? No, but she does gain an insight into the terrible ennui that afflicts her. Now she must leave.

Or...

> Can Bill break into the abandoned warehouse? Yes, but there is a dead body! Now he must cover his tracks.

If this seems like a step into too much detail, I can only say give it a go. It saves me time *and* inspires my imagination.

How to write a Scene QABN

If you have a good Chapter outline, it's really, really easy to find a satisfying Scene QABN. Remember we said:
o A chapter (a) must contain at least one *clash* between moves, and (b) the final move must create suspense.

There's no simple one-to-one correspondence between the moves and the elements of the QABN. It's like making bread. The chapter's moves are ingredients, but the chapter itself is a lump of dough. Whatever tells the story is fine.

However, if you are of a geeky mindset like me, then the following might help.
o If the final move of the chapter is a *surprise move* of some kind, i.e. an event that won't have much wordcount, then it belongs in the But and implies the Now.

For example:

```
Lukan tries to arrest them x ND evade and
get   home   x   RG   have   already   taken
possession!
```

Becomes:

Can the New Dockers evade Lukan? Yes, but Leander feels jaded and the Rival Gang have taken their home. Now they must fight for their existence.

Yes, I gave Jaded Leader a name and this chapter contains just one scene. Also, note that the QABN form is the servant not the master. In this case, there are two buts: (1) Leander becomes jaded, which I drew from elsewhere in the outline; (2) Rival Gang have claim-jumped.

Not all chapters end on surprises! Some end on winning moves. That's OK:

- If the final move of the chapter is the *winning move* of a clash between moves, then the implied suspense belongs in the But Now.

    Staying with *Barbarian in the City*, the next chapter has:

    > Cador saves ND. C offers to hire ND x members suspicious x seeing his own advantage, jaded leader convinces them. NDs want to strike against ODs x intent on pleasing C, jaded leader directs them to easy targets.

    The winning move—" x intent on pleasing C, jaded leader directs them to easy targets"—points to the suspense, so we get:

    > Will the gang go after the Old Dockers? No, Leander persuades them to go for softer targets. However, this is really because he has switched allegiance to Cador. Now he will pursue his own advantage.

    However, this leaves the rest of the chapter. No problem, just work backwards applying the same magic. The end result looks like this:

    > Can the New Dockers defeat Rival Gang? No, but Cador saves them. Now they must deal with a sorcerer.
    >
    > Can Cador hire the New Dockers? Yes, but only because the jaded Leander sees his own advantage. Now Leander must maintain two faces.
    >
    > Will the gang go after the Old Dockers? No, Leander persuades them to go for softer targets. However, this is really because he has switched allegiance to Cador. Now he will pursue his own advantage.

Oops! This chapter turns out to have three scenes. Perhaps it will end up as more than one chapter.

Debate Scenes

So this scene...

> Will the gang go after the Old Dockers? No, Leander persuades them to go for softer targets. However, this is really because he has switched allegiance to Cador. Now he will pursue his own advantage.

...brings us to what some people call the "sequel" or "transition" scene. I don't like either term much. One merely implies what happened, and the other housekeeping and sightseeing (yawn). Of course, this kind of scene is useful because it does both, and also slows down the pace. However, it still has a driving conflict: *characters versus decision.*

So, let's call it what it is, a Debate Scene.

Debate Scenes need not involve 3rd parties. For example, my Story Outline might say:

> Trying to reach a decision, Eric wanders his hometown, each sight tugging at conflicting memories. He arrives at his old school and decides: time to go after the monster!

The Chapter Outline would have:

> His hometown depresses Eric x the sight of his old school sends him after the monster.

Or, if we were feeling lazy or had Eric firmly in our head:

> Eric reluctantly decides to go after the monster.

Regardless, the resulting QABN is the same:

> *Will Eric go after the monster despite hating his hometown?* Yes, but only because his old school reminds him of childhood innocence. Now he needs guns, lots of guns. Or perhaps a flamethrower.

Don't neglect Debate Scenes. Apart from nicely doubling your wordcount and improving your pacing, they also give you an opportunity to really explore your world and your characters and put in all the quirky stuff you learned how to do in writing workshops.

Also, remember that a Debate Scene can be a testosterone-fuelled confrontation:

> Richard the Lionheart accuses William of trying to kill him x William persuades him to make him Earl of Pembroke.

Giving us:

> *Can William survive a confrontation with the angry and generally murderous king whose horse he killed?* Yes, but actually he manages to wangle marriage with an heiress. Now he must deal with the responsibilities of being the Earl of Pembroke and his old life as knight errant is over.

Final thoughts: Parallel narratives

Visualise your scenes, but don't worry too much about how you will write them. For example, if a battle has scenes from different characters overlapping in time, that's fine. You can chop them up and interweave them to show different character experiences as they happen.

It's only worth doing a handful of Scene QABNs at a time because the act of storytelling tends to change the story. Once you have these, it's time to do some Scene Outlines.

Worldbuilding with Scene QABNs

Sometimes—often—you can't quite get a Scene QABN out of a couple of moves in a Chapter Outline. That's fine. This is where you make something up or research it. If that something is to do with culture, history or some other aspect of your story world, then you are worldbuilding.

For example, from a barbarian romp:

```
Kthar confronts Riltar but neither backs
down. Both go off to raise armies.
```

Gives us:

```
Can Kthar overawe Riltar? No. But…. Now
they go off to raise armies.
```

Where's the But? How about,

```
Can Kthar overawe Riltar? No. But, nor can
he finish the matter since he cannot shed
blood during the Festival of R'Ungr. Now
they   go   off  to   raise   armies   and
destructive war is inevitable.
```

Suddenly this is more vivid. Obviously, our hero has chosen the wrong moment to confront his rival, who will now have time to go off and raise an army.

Scene QABNs Exercises

o Take one of the chapter outlines you produced (see **"Chapter Outline Exercise"** on page 70) and create several scene questions using the QABN format.

Scene Outlines

But wait, there's more!

Yes, sorry; I'm sure you are itching to just write but there's one more tool you might need. It's what stops me getting lost when I actually draft a scene: a Scene Outline. You do it pretty much the way you do Chapter Outlines, except you get to write in flow.

How to write a Scene Outline

For example, we had:

> *Can the New Dockers evade Lukan?* Yes, but Leander feels jaded. Worse, the Rival Gang have taken their home. Now they must fight for their existence.

From which, writing off the top of my head, I get:

> NDs escape into the old warehouse x spotted by watchman (security recently improved)
>
> Leg it x watchman chases
>
> Leander could run x feels too old
>
> Leander knifes watchman x more watchmen turn up
>
> To the street! X Now Captain Lukan is in pursuit
>
> Take to a side alley x Lukan and men dismount and follow
>
> Abandon a wounded comrade x still following
>
> Take to old sewer x still following

> UP Ladder where gang can drop rocks on pursuers x Captain Lukan: I get you next time!
>
> NG taunt x get back to base and find Rival Gang in possession.
>
> NGs in dismay x Leander suddenly realises he doesn't care about them; due to turnover, all strangers.
>
> Leander would like to walk away x nowhere to go
>
> NGs nervous x Leander persuades them they have a home ground advantage
>
> L knows there will be body count x if he has a base then he can build a new gang.

I hope you can immediately see several advantages. First, you get to just tell the story; no messing with nice words, or worrying about repetition, voice or other literary concerns.

Second, you get to handle the practicalities of cause and effect... the *choreography*... before you invest in fine prose. Suppose I decide the sewer is a cliché and bin the scene? I'd have sacrificed just 159 words, rather than two or three *thousand*.

Third and last, you get to *see* what's ahead. That will make the writing smoother, and the situation-painting more convincing. If a ladder *up* is vital to the escape, then let's have the gang pass rusting rungs and broken ladders before they find the one they want. Also, you can set up complications for the characters. For example, if you know the only exit is going to be an old ladder, why not give one of the likable characters a broken ankle?

Once you have an outline, you can finally draft the text. Needless to say, I have something to say about that too!

Worldbuilding in the Scene Outline

At this point, most of your worldbuilding should be done!

However, during outlining you may learn new things about your setting, or encounter new people. That's fine and part of the fun. Add them to your notes.

Scene Outlines Exercises

o Take one of the Scene QABNs you produced (see "**Scene QABNs Exercises**" on page 75) and create/rough out a scene outline.
O Make up a totally bonkers Scene QABN and outline that. (Extra points for including ninja mermaids.)

Storytelling Tools: Summary

o The three Storytelling tools are similar to the Story Sculpting ones. Use them in any order, and jump between them (and to Story Sculpting!) as required.
o The Chapter Outline establishes the chapters. Each must at least contain a clash between opposing moves. It must also end with suspense, typically either a surprise or a winning move with implications.
o The Scene QABNs capture the purpose and direction of each scene.
O The Scene Outlines make each scene easily draftable.

Storytelling Tools: Exercises

o If you haven't already, use some of the material you created for earlier exercises to create a Chapter Outline plus Scene QABNs and Scene Outlines for the first few chapters.

6. DRAFTING THE TEXT

Story Sculpting	Storytelling
Conflict Diagrams	Chapter Outline
Story QABNs	Scene QABNs
Story Outlines	Scene Outlines
TEXT	

At last it's time to write actual words the reader will—*may*—see.

In a typical five-hour writing day, I can manage 2.5K words. It doesn't sound that impressive until I add that my text usually requires just one extra pass, not redraft or revision, to be "editor ready". (If you don't have an editor, I guess that takes you to two extra passes.)

Though writers, especially novices, get hung up on daily wordcount, what really matters is *average* daily wordcount. Sure, if you churn out 7K words today that's impressive; less impressive if you spend the next 10 writing days editing them.

It follows that what you really want to produce is *good* words that are *easy to edit*. All the tools I've described will help you with this. However, there's one technique that I find pretty decisive in my quest for creative productivity.

The World/Character Dialogue

This is my super secret ninja productivity tool, so I'll just go right ahead and describe it. The World/Character Dialogue works like this:

```
WORLD [Paragraph of external events seen
from the character's point-of-view and
described using their voice.]

CHARACTER [Paragraph from the character's
```

> point of view, beginning with visceral reactions, working through physical reactions and ending in speech or thought.]

That *looks* complicated, but really it's just your point-of-view character in dialogue with the external world.

> Bullets punched through the door, sprayed splinters into the room. Blood splashed from Horsa's chest, spattered the wall behind him.
>
> Hengest dived for cover, rolled behind a control console, brought up his AK47 and let fly a three-round burst. "You killed my friend, you bastards!"

Or...

> Steam spiralled dreamily from the surface of the herbal tea, just like the smoke from the peat fire at that rented Highland cottage last year where Jocasta had been happy for the first and last time.
>
> Jocasta sighed and hunched over her book. Life went on, but not for her.

It doesn't always have to be paragraphs. Sometimes you end up with sentences or even clauses. Take that paragraph I served up when we were talking about "Snipers in the Belfries". Here it is broken with the World parts in italics:

> *A movement on the roof* drew Olaf's eye. He squinted into the glare and frowned. *The sun had turned the forest of belfries into jagged silhouettes.* What with all those gargoyles and ornamental projections, there was no way of knowing how many snipers were up there. He toggled his communicator. "Air strike at the following coordinates."

It's still a dialogue, and I often write like this. However, the best way of learning the technique is to think in terms of paragraphs of dialogue, so I shall stick to that.

Prerequisites for using World/Character Dialogue

There's slightly more to say about this technique, but I'm making some assumptions about the basics of how you are writing. The World/Character Dialogue works best if you are writing in the following manner:

o **Narrative Mode**: You are using third person ("He/she did this") or first person ("I did this") such that the reader *only* experiences and sees what the Point of View does, i.e. "Close Third Person" or (there doesn't seem to be a term for it) plain First Person. If you like whimsical digressions and authorial intrusions, Olympian viewpoint and so on, that's great, but I am not sure that this section will help you.

o **Point-Of-View Character:** You are using one focal, i.e. "point-of-view" character, per scene. We tend to call this the "POV Character".

o **Tense**: (Shrug) Use something sensible; present tense works for some subgenres, otherwise past tense is your friend.

How to use the World/Character Dialogue

So, assuming we're on the same page, let's break up the World/Character Dialogue and look at how to use it effectively.

World Paragraphs encompass anything external to the POV Character's mind, *including* their body; however, what they describe is still (a) subjective to that character and (b) uses their voice, i.e. only that language and imagery available to them.

Let's look at *subjectivity* first. For example:

```
Some hippy girls in cheerful clothing—all
embroidered swirls and colourful patches—
```

> wandered over. The tallest, a young woman of about twenty with wild hennaed hair, raised her hand. "Hi! Did you see the aliens?"

Now, same action, different POV Character:

> Some sluts in garish clothing slunk over. The tallest, an unkempt doxy with dyed hair raised a dirty paw. "Hi!" she drawled. "Did you see the aliens?"

What's nice is that World Paragraphs are written as if they are objective, but really contain all the obsessions and prejudices of the POV Character. This is an incredibly useful feature, especially when using third person, because you can suck the reader into their world, no matter how uncomfortable.

Where subjectivity tells us about the character, *voice* tells us about their world. For example…

> The brawler steamed through the bar, bulldozing through the other fighters, fists working like pile-drivers.

…tells us that the POV Character is a denizen of Industrial Age, probably not a soldier.

Same action, different POV Character:

> The brawler bulled through the tavern, tossing aside the other fighters, fists like battering rams.

Pre-modern, right? Some culture with siege warfare. Possibly the POV Character has seen war.

You can also change the pacing and level of detail by pushing more into the World Paragraphs, especially during what I've called Debate Scenes (also known as "transitions" or "sequels"):

> Jane sidestepped a couple of drunks, stepped over a dog, body-swerved around a lecherous lordling and finally made it to the back of the tavern.

This kind of narrative summary really belongs in a World Paragraph because it's really just describing a situation which she will shortly react to in her Character Paragraph.

Notice that there is no "filtering", no "he saw/felt/heard". The only times I might put that in are (a) at the very start of a chapter or scene so the reader knows what's going on:

> William backed away as the brawler steamed towards him through the bar, bulldozing through the other fighters, fists working like pile-drivers.

And, (b) when the POV Character is obnoxious to modern morality, and my editor doesn't want some arse to quote me out of context:

> The tallest, a hot babe with bedroom hair raised her hand. Bangles covered her forearm from wrist to elbow. Jayce pictured her leaving them on in the sack. "Hi!" she drawled. "Did you see the aliens?"

Character Paragraphs describe the POV Character's reactions in strict chronological order. This usually means working from the instinctive, unconscious to the conscious and, finally, the verbal.

> Jayce's jaw dropped. These were like the girls he'd seen on the Woodstock documentary. If he played along, perhaps he'd get lucky. "Sure I did."

Or...

> William's fingers tightened on his sword pommel. A sick feeling welled up in his stomach. He drew the sword and put the point against the wizard's throat with a single fluid action. "Where is my spaceship, warlock?"

The end result is very easy to write, not least because you are not trying to find elegant joining phrases (which you will later cut out anyway) and always produces clear prose. Better still, because action and reaction are not tangled—it's almost modular!—the resulting text is very easy to edit, and to expand or contract.

Editing, Expanding and Contracting World/Character Dialogs

For example, take Jayce and the Hippies. The relevant part of the Scene Outline read:

```
Hippy Girls try to warn Jayce x He thinks
they're stoned and plans to seduce one or
more of them.
```

The resulting draft could read:

```
Some hippy girls in dippy clothing—all
embroidered swirls and colourful patches—
wandered over. The tallest, a babe of
about twenty with wild hennaed hair,
raised her hand. "Hi! Did you see the
aliens?"

Jayce's jaw dropped. These were like the
girls he'd seen on the Woodstock
documentary. "Sure I did."
```

However, it could be much shorter...

```
Some hippy chicks wandered over. The
tallest raised her hand. "Hi! Did you see
the aliens?"

Jayce's jaw dropped. "Sure I did."
```

And it could be made longer, either as drafted, or else by redrafting, breaking up each paragraph into a WP/CP pair:

```
Some hippy chicks in cheerful clothing—all
    embroidered swirls and colourful patches—
```

```
swayed over, a fluid swing in their hips
that drew the eye.

Jayce's jaw dropped. These were like the
girls he'd seen on the Woodstock
documentary. He took a step their way and
tried to work out whether they were
wearing underwear.

The tallest, a hot babe with bedroom hair,
raised her hand. Bangles covered her
forearm from wrist to elbow. She probably
left them on in the sack. "Hi!" she
drawled. "Did you see the aliens?"

Jayce grinned and stared down her
cleavage. Stoned out of her gourd, he
realised. "Why, yes," he said. "I did see
the aliens."
```

Really, it's that easy! At first, writing this way can feel a little artificial. However, you as soon as you get into the rhythm it will feel as natural as breathing.

Worldbuilding during drafting

There'll always be little details to add when you write. If they seem important, jot them down somewhere, e.g. make of gun or car or handbag.

However, researching or detailed Worldbuilding tends to cause drafting to grind to a halt. Don't be afraid just to use a placeholder and come back later when you are not in flow. For example:

```
Jayce drew his XXXBIG GUNXXXX and pulled
the trigger.

XXXSPECIAL EFFECTXXX the wall crumbled.
The girls screamed and dived for cover.

Jayce spat. "Damned aliens!"
```

Remember, nobody is looking over your shoulder, nobody is criticising as you write. If and when your novel is published and hits the e-readers and bookshelves, people will admire your vivid imagination and attention to detail. They'll picture you hammering out the tale all at one go. That's all that matters.

Drafting: Summary

o Draft using a World/Character dialogue, typically in paired paragraphs.

Drafting Exercises

o Make up a bizarre situation and try free-writing using World Paragraphs and Character Paragraphs.
o Take one of the scenes you outlined and write it.
o Now write your novel.

7. FINAL WORD

There's a hell of a lot more to writing professionally, and even more to doing it creatively.

However, this is just a short handbook—though it may grow as I gather experience.

If you have any questions or insights to share, please drop by my blog at **www.mharoldpage.com**, where you'll also find out about my latest books.

Good luck!

M Harold Page
www.mharoldpage.com

Printed in Great Britain
by Amazon